CHRISTIAN DEVOTION

CHRISTIAN DEVOTION

Addresses by
JOHN BAILLIE

CHARLES SCRIBNER'S SONS
New York

Library of Congress Catalog Card Number 62-17723

FOREWORD

It would be ungracious to let this small volume of my husband's sermons go to press without expressing my profound thanks to Professor John McIntyre, D.D., of New College, Edinburgh, for his abundant help. He not only gave much time to reading them and making a selection from a large number, but also kindly corrected the proofs. Without his generous assistance, and the wise counsels of Mrs. Forrester, this little book would never have been published.

F. JEWEL BAILLIE

Edinburgh, 1961

CONTENTS

A COUSIN'S MEMORIES

JOHN BAILLIE died on 29 September 1960, and it is too early
for the story of his crowded life to be adequately written.
But these memories may be of some interest to people who
read this and others of his books and would like to know a
little about the writer.

The Free Church Manse of Gairloch, where John Baillie
was born in the year 1886, stands above the white sands of
one of the loveliest bays in Wester Ross. Today one can
hardly imagine how isolated from the life of the world outside was the little community of Gaelic-speaking crofters and
fisher-folk to which John Baillie's father ministered. Even the
town of Inverness was a whole day's journey away. Indeed
the people of Gairloch had easier communication by sea with
the Hebridean islands to the west of them, and their Gaelic
speech and Gaelic culture were little affected by modern in-
fluences. John Baillie to the end of his life could recall some
of the Gaelic psalms and Gaelic phrases he had learned as a
child, and his speech never lost the soft Highland lilt.

In these Highland communities the minister, with his book-
learning, his knowledge of the outside world, and his spiritual
authority, was greatly revered, and even among Highland
ministers the Rev. John Baillie of Gairloch was remarkable.
Nearly fifty years after his death a crofter's wife could recall

"a sermon I heard Mr. Baillie preach at a baptism, when I was a child." "A divine of strong character and courtly bearing," his Calvinism was of the most rigorous kind, and he saw to it that the whole life of the community was imbued with the theology of the Westminster Confession. One of his son's earliest memories was of sitting on his father's knee, in front of the nursery fire, giving "with perfect readiness" the correct answer to the still incomprehensible question, "What is the chief end of man?" And another childish memory was of the wide natural amphitheatre, known in Gaelic as "The Bed of the White Cow," where crowds gathered in solemn awe at the yearly "communion season," and the holiness and the mercy of God came like a wind upon the souls of men.

The Free Church minister late in life married a young widow, Annie Macpherson of Gairloch, and when he died six years later there were three little sons in the manse. John, the eldest, was only five when he lost his father, but to the end of his life he remained certain that his own Christian pilgrimage had its beginning in the manse of Gairloch and in his father's influence. "Actually the way he lived, and the kind of being he was, exercised over me a more powerful and lasting constraint than all his spoken words of command." [1]

The young widow, left with a very meagre income and the sole responsibility for the future of her three little boys, had no doubt at all as to what that future would be. They were all to follow in their father's footsteps as ministers of the Gospel, and in His own good way God would provide for them. "He will bless the house of Aaron," she used constantly to say. She arranged to leave her native Gairloch and she found a little house in Inverness where the boys could begin

[1] *Invitation to Pilgrimage*, p. 38.

the long course of education necessary. She joined the Free North Church, where the Faith was preached as her husband had preached it, and she herself continued the religious training in the home as her husband would have wished. John long afterwards testified to his mother's grasp of the intricacies of Calvinist theology, and wrote, "If her sons later developed any aptitudes of a philosophic kind, it was undoubtedly by this home training in theological dialectic that their minds were first sharpened." She gathered round herself and her boys a small circle of like-minded friends, and she contrived that the little house should always seem a place of warmth and cheer. *How* she loved to justify some small extravagance in welcoming friends by quoting a Gaelic proverb, "It's not every day that the Mackintosh keeps court!" She bought "bolts" of tweed and "bolts" of flannel, out of which she fashioned the clothes in which her little sons went to Church and school. And in due course she arranged for each boy in turn to begin his formal education at the Royal Academy, Inverness, a school with a history of seven hundred years, which had some outstanding masters and many boys of remarkable promise.

Of the effect of Inverness Academy on boys steeped in Calvinism, John writes vividly in his brief memoir of his brother, Donald.[1] Their minds at school were set afire by Shakespeare—"But there was no room at all for Shakespeare within the Puritanism of our early upbringing." They were trained to distinguish fact from legend—"But our training at home did not allow us to practise this skill on the Bible stories." They were introduced to the world-view of modern science—"But we could not make it square into the up-and-

[1] Contained in the volume, *The Theology of the Sacraments* by Donald M. Baillie, (1957).

down, three-storey, geocentric universe of the Bible writers."
It was no wonder that before the end of their school days
both John and Donald experienced the spiritual strain of trying to reconcile the old and the new in their education. But
neither confessed it to the other through a sensitive fear of
disturbing his faith. The apologia for Christianity which the
mature John Baillie was able to offer so persuasively had to
be wrought out through years of recurring intellectual dis-
tress. Yet it seems that neither John nor Donald ever contemplated any change of vocation, and, while they fought
their doubts, they went steadily on with their preparation for
the ministry.

By the end of his school days, John's outstanding ability
was clear. He was "Dux" of the school, president of its debat-
ing society, and, with Donald, the centre of a group of very
able boys.

And now his mother proceeded to the next stage of her
plan. John went to Edinburgh to live in "digs" as a university
student, and a year later, when Donald too had finished his
schooling, the whole family moved to Edinburgh. Peter was
now committed to becoming a medical missionary, and in
due course followed his brothers to the university. A little
house was found in a Morningside crescent, where a small
room was shared as a study by the three brothers—so small a
room that it was a momentous event when a new bookcase
had to be fitted in! In that room John laid the foundations of
his philosophical and theological learning, and incidentally
from Peter's text-books picked up a knowledge of medicine
which made his doctors in later life treat him with consider-
able respect. Dr. Sydney Price, friend and doctor in his later
years in Edinburgh, used to say that a professional visit to
John was almost as alarming as a degree examination!

The "Dux" of Inverness Academy became the medallist of the philosophy classes in Edinburgh University, as did Donald a year later. Each in turn was appointed assistant to the Professor of Moral Philosophy, and each in turn proceeded to New College, Edinburgh, for the four years' course of preparation for the ministry of the United Free Church. There too "the Baillie brothers" became legendary for their brilliance, and gathered round them a group of outstanding young men. About some of those who subsequently died in battle John writes in his memoir of Donald with that affectionate and astonished delight in the qualities of his friends which was one of his endearing characteristics. The common room of New College, the paths over the Pentland Hills, and perhaps most of all the little house in Braidburn Crescent, were the setting for their discussion and argument, their nonsense and laughter, their new discoveries in the realm of ideas and their support for each other in the difficult quest for full faith. John recalls in one of his latest books [1] how as a student he walked home one frosty midnight after a discussion on the existence of God and stopped to gaze into the starry sky— "Into these deep immensities I hurled my despairing question, but it seemed like nothing and no answer came back."

The divinity students of that time in Edinburgh were privileged in their teachers—men like Alexander Whyte, at once Puritan, Catholic and saint, H. R. Mackintosh, H. A. A. Kennedy and A. R. MacEwen—and in the preaching they could hear in the great churches of the city. John and his friends would sometimes desert their own churches of a Sunday evening to stand in the queue outside Free St. George's for the joy of listening to the beloved and gallant John Kelman, or to slip into the much emptier St. Andrew's

[1] *The Idea of Revelation in Recent Thought* (1956), p. 138.

Drumsheugh (whose aristocratic congregation dined at seven!) to hear the superb sermons of W. M. Macgregor, that preacher to preachers, disturber of consciences, and whetstone of minds.

During his years at New College John spent two summers of study in Germany—at Jena and Marburg. And then, his academic honours thick upon him, he made his own early experiments in preaching to somewhat bewildered congregations in Broughton Place Church, Edinburgh, where he was assistant for two years. In later life he delighted to tell how he began one of his early sermons with some such sentence as this, "Our forefathers were wont to speak of the True Faith and the false faiths: today it is more natural for us to speak of higher and lower forms of religion." As the congregation "skailed" at the end of the service, one old woman was overheard asking another, "What thocht ye o' thon?" To which the reply was emphatic, "A heard only the first sentence and A thankit my Maker A was too deaf to hear ony mair."

It was in the years in Edinburgh when good scholarships had brought more freedom in the use of money that John began to discover the realm of Art. There was no place at all for it in his Highland upbringing, but it was now to become a very important part of his life, and an Easter vacation in Holland with Donald and a friend was the first of the many holidays he spent exploring the treasures of Europe. By middle life he had developed a connoisseur's appreciation of pictures and architecture, and his home was full of small and lovely things he had found on his travels.

By 1914 Mrs. Baillie must have felt that God had blessed her efforts beyond all her hopes. John and Donald stood at the beginning of their service as ministers of the Gospel, and early in that year Peter sailed for India as a medical missionary. Her influence had shaped and moulded her sons in their earlier years, and now in turn they were influencing her, opening to her new interests and new enjoyments and a fuller Christian liberty. At the Christmas parties shared with two families of cousins, where ludicrous charades were always staged, she would watch her boys decked in her own bonnets, impersonating incredible characters, and her eyes would twinkle with amusement and pride, even while her soft Highland voice strove to make itself heard through the laughter, "Now, John! Now, Donnie! Now, Peter! That's enough. Don't go too far!"

In May 1914 the tragic news came from India that Peter Baillie, along with another young missionary, had been drowned while still at language school. The blow to his mother was shattering, and John and Donald ministered to her with great tenderness until slowly her faith in God's providence was renewed and deepened and she could take up life again. Then came the outbreak of war in August, cutting across all their planned future. Many of their friends volunteered for combatant service, but for John with his grateful memories of study in Germany and his independence of judgment the issues were not as clearly-cut as they seemed to most of his generation, and at first he believed it to be his duty to continue with his work as a minister. But later he felt impelled to offer for service with the Y.M.C.A., and he was for a large part of the war years in France, occupied in educational work for the troops, sharing some of their risks and hardships, and discovering among them "a most remarkable and hardly-to-be-exaggerated sense of reality, and for the difference between reality and sham" [1] which was to prove a powerful influence on his own teaching later.

[1] *Roots of Religion in the Human Soul* (1926), p. 4.

At Boulogne in 1916 he met the girl who was to become his wife and to share so fully in his interests and friendships and journeyings. Jewel Fowler, a descendant of the famous Elizabethan Bishop Jewel, was also working with the Y.M.C.A. A year later they became engaged, and were married in 1919, shortly before John was released from the Y.M.C.A.

In the first months of their married life a choice had to be made between invitations to different kinds of work in Scotland and in America. The momentous decision was taken to accept the offer of the Chair of Christian Theology in Auburn Theological Seminary, New York State, and so it came to pass that for the rest of his life John—and no less his wife—in a very real sense belonged to two continents. He used to say that when people asked him on trans-Atlantic crossings whether he was British or American, he had to reply "Well! I think I'm really half and half!" And on John's lips the statement was self-evident, for he always gave to the first "half" a broad sonorous â worthy of any Oxford don, while he clipped and flattened the second "half" to the accent of Broadway.

Eight years were spent at Auburn, where their only son, Ian, was born, and three years at Emmanuel College, Toronto, followed. With few responsibilities in church or community John was able to recover his old habits of study. He was an adoring father, but even against small Ian his study door was locked from nine to one each day. In these years he wrote and published his first three books, *The Roots of Religion in the Human Soul*, *The Interpretation of Religion*, and *The Place of Jesus Christ in Modern Christianity*, the last of which became known to an unusually wide public through being chosen as a "Book of the Month" by the Religious Book Club.

In 1930 he was appointed to the Roosevelt Chair of Systematic Theology in Union Theological Seminary, New York. The four years he and his wife spent there were among the most stimulating and fruitful of their lives. John was in the fulness of his powers, well-known as a preacher and lecturer, and bearing the doctorates of Divinity of Edinburgh and Toronto. The life of New York was excitingly congenial to them both, and on the staff and among the students of Union they quickly made firm friends. Reinhold Niebuhr was then a young professor, and the brilliant Ursula Keppel-Compton had just arrived from England to study theology. "You *must* take Professor Niebuhr's classes," John advised her, "You'll love him." Which she did! Reinhold and Ursula Niebuhr, Henry and Dorothy Coffin and Pitney and Betty Van Dusen (the "Six in New York" to whom John dedicated his *Invitation to Pilgrimage*), with Paul and Lilie Scherer and others shared with John and Jewel Baillie a life of great vitality and warm friendship. And in New York, John, whose liberal views in his student days had occasionally alarmed his professors, found himself considered a champion of orthodoxy. "He somewhat astonished his pupils by his faith in the Christian religion" said the Promoter when the honorary degree of D.D. was conferred on John by Yale in 1934! It was in Union Seminary that his book on the Christian hope of immortality, *And the Life Everlasting*, was wrought out, and it was there that "its affirmations were uttered with unforgettable conviction and power." (His mother had died in 1933 and the book is dedicated "*In memoriam matris dilectissimæ.*")

John returned to Scotland as Professor of Divinity in Edinburgh University in 1934, and in the same year Donald was appointed to the Chair of Systematic Theology in St. Andrews. For the next twenty years the "Baillie Brothers" exercised an immense influence upon the thinking youth of Scotland. They had both been deeply affected by Barth's influence, but neither had accepted his system as a whole. Bishop Stephen Neill in his recent book on *Twentieth Century Christianity* recalls that while John Baillie in America had to challenge too simple forms of liberalism, "in Scotland he fought against a too worshipful acceptance of Barth's system." John took whimsical pleasure in noticing how his critics now attacked him from another quarter, and he enjoyed at least as much as its author a ribald student rhyme which began:

> Baillie, Baillie, give me an answer do.
> Why ain't Plato found in the Canon too?

His theological students and the many others of different faculties who heard him speak at meetings and conferences of the Student Christian Movement delighted in his wit and wisdom and discovered his concern for them as people. Year by year Americans crossed the Atlantic to study under him, and were welcomed not only in his class-room, but in the spacious friendly home which he and his wife established at 9 Whitehouse Terrace. Students from many parts of the world carried away grateful memories of parties with wonderful talk and wonderful food and old-fashioned parlour games with an intellectual twist to them, and of John and Jewel Baillie as the kindest of hosts.

John's work as a teacher had always first claim on him, but in these years after his return to Scotland he began to be much in demand as a preacher and to be drawn into public life. People discovered his willingness to support pioneering ventures of faith before they had proved themselves, and from the beginning of the Iona Community he and Donald were among the official sponsors and stood shoulder to shoulder with George Macleod in many of his early battles. John was invited by Dr. J. H. Oldham to join the remarkable discussion group known as "The Moot", where people of ability in many different fields found stimulus in grappling together with the most urgent problems of the day. Indeed, John's fertility of thought throughout his life owed much to this kind of stimulus by his peers—and most of all to the stimulus of his brother Donald. Theirs was a wonderful relationship in which each genuinely esteemed the other better than himself, and in which the qualities of each complemented those of the other. Their discussions often turned into the passionate arguments beloved of Highlanders, but their love grew only the deeper.

It is to this period that *A Diary of Private Prayer* belongs: it was published in 1936 "For Ian", then a schoolboy of fifteen. Every year since then the little book has reached a wider public, and by the time of John's death almost 400,000 copies had been sold in the American and English editions, and translations into at least thirteen other languages had been made. John never ceased to be touched by the letters which constantly reached him from unknown men and women thanking him for the way in which *A Diary of Private Prayer* had led them into the very presence of God.

After the outbreak of war in 1939 when colleges were depleted of their students, the Y.M.C.A. once more secured John's services, and in February 1940 he crossed to France to take charge of all the educational and religious work for the troops. His plans were just beginning to take shape when the break-through of the Germans in May suddenly brought the middle-aged professor of theology into the thick of events. In the confusion and constant danger of the following weeks he arranged for the safety of the Y.M.C.A. staff (though all stores had to be abandoned) and only then did he, his driver and an elderly colleague seek their own escape. They headed south with the pitiful torrents of refugees and broken troop units, exposed to bombing and machine-gunning from the air. They were so often hungry that when needed food was found, there would come into John's mind the psalm he had learned as a child:

> My table Thou hast furnished
> In presence of my foes.

At last St. Malo was reached and with over two thousand three hundred people they were crowded on to a little motor vessel to return to England. Through those weeks when in the absence of news from home it seemed increasingly certain that final defeat had come to the Allies, John kept his usual careful record of each day's events, he planned for his friends and fellow-workers, and he took services for the troops.

Out of the maelstrom he returned to Scotland with a sure word of faith. Bewildered people turned to him for guidance, and from many pulpits he preached "to their condition," simply, realistically and with quiet confidence. The Church of Scotland appointed him convener of a commission of its ablest men "for the Interpretation of God's Will in the Present Crisis," and the reports presented in successive years from 1941 to 1945 did much to direct and steady the thinking of Christian people in Scotland and in other parts of the world. In America too he played a part in the shaping of public opinion when he crossed the Atlantic in 1941 to speak about the war. Through his friend Reinhold Niebuhr he had been kept in close touch with American thought, and on that visit he did much to present the issues at stake and to win sympathy for the Allied cause. And astonishingly in the same year he delivered in Glasgow those most persuasive of his lectures on the Christian faith, later published as *Invitation to Pilgrimage*.

In 1943 John was elected Moderator of the General Assembly of the Church of Scotland. Because of his Highland ancestry it was arranged that during his year of office he should visit many of the remoter presbyteries of the north and west. There in isolated manses lonely ministers, bewildered by the shaking of Europe, welcomed him with almost tearful joy as reporter and interpreter and prophet, and often kept him talking half the night by their study fires.

The war was scarcely over before John paid a visit to Germany with a small delegation of British churchmen to renew contact with the churches there. This proved to be a very important visit, both in renewal of personal friendships, and in the information and guidance made available for the Allied Control Commission and for the British Council of Churches. A similar visit to Norway followed. A less exacting and more enjoyable piece of public service was a visit to New Zealand in 1948 when he represented both the Church of Scotland and the University of Edinburgh at the centenary celebrations in Dunedin. This time he and his wife made a long trip of it, visiting Australia first and adding a lecturing tour in America afterwards.

In spite of these and many other public claims upon him, John with his superb self-discipline in the use of time and energy never allowed his academic work to suffer. In 1950 he was appointed Principal of New College and Dean of the Faculty of Divinity and he carried a heavy load of administrative responsibility from then until his retirement in 1956.

His retirement was an event to which he jestingly said he had looked forward all his life, and he celebrated it by returning with his wife for a very happy winter in Union Seminary, New York, as Fosdick Visiting Professor. It was among his old friends there that he received the news of the crowning honour of his life—his appointment by the Queen as a Companion of Honour. John had many honorary degrees, but this royal recognition of his public service gave a quite peculiar pleasure to him and his wife, as to their friends.

What can be said in the space that remains about what was perhaps the greatest achievement of John's life as it was certainly the major interest of his last years—his service to the Ecumenical Movement? He was one of the young stewards at "Edinburgh, 1910"; an active worker in the Faith and Order Movement from the early thirties; a member of the British Council of Churches almost from its foundation; at the first Assembly of the World Council of Churches elected a member of its Central Committee; and at the second Assembly at Evanston appointed one of the six World Presidents. These bare facts can do no more than suggest what he contributed in vision, in wisdom, in constant travel, in administrative ability, in prayer and in a great wealth of personal friendships to the drawing together of the separated parts of Christ's Church on earth. It was a deep disappointment to him that his own church rejected the recommendations of the "Report on Conversations between Anglican and Presbyterian Churches," which he himself had helped to frame, but he never allowed his disappointment to affect his personal relationships in the present or his hope for the future. In all he said and did in his later years it was clear that, as Hugh Montefiore wrote about Donald, he "was not just a Presbyterian Divine: like all the saints he belongs to the whole Church of God."

The range and variety of John's interests made him an inveterate traveller by land and sea and air, and to his many friends in many lands he must have seemed utterly at home in their conference-halls, lecture-rooms and pulpits, and at their tables and by their firesides. But for those who knew him in his own home in Edinburgh, the most vivid memories of John are set in his study there, that grave book-lined room, with windows shadowed in summer by the trees of the big garden. It was a quiet room, with the noises of our modern world kept outside—no telephone, no radio, no typewriter. And it was a room with three clear focal points. There was the big uncluttered desk by the window where John sat for many hours of the day writing, in his clear beautiful handwriting, sermons, lectures and articles, and dealing punctiliously and courteously with the endless stream of letters which came, asking him to preach, to lecture, to advise. He disliked accepting an invitation to speak until he had, at least in outline, an idea of what he would say but, even so, his replies would be as promptly despatched as those of lesser mortals.

And there was, as another focal point, the big leather chair, where he often sat far into the night reading—the innumerable reports and periodicals which came to him from many quarters, the most recent books of theology and philosophy, novels, poetry, biography, all seasoned (like the reading of many theologians) with a reasonable sprinkling of good "detectives."

From chair or desk he would leap to his feet to welcome

his visitors, with the outstretched hand and quick look of real pleasure which tempted them to forget how busy a man he was. His old students came back to ask him to recommend them for new posts (John often saw in his old students possibilities which no one else could detect, and almost invariably he was right). They wanted him to write introductions to their books. They wanted him to advise them about their vocations for, as one wrote after his death, "the adventurous act of obedience could be sure to find sensitive understanding in him." Missionaries, and church leaders and theologians of many communions came to talk through their problems with him. And old friends and new came just to be warmed by his friendship.

To welcome these many visitors he would start from desk or chair. But there was a third focal point in that quiet room —the prayer-desk by the window with its little pile of well-worn versions of the Scriptures and of devotional books. There, at the times when he was sure to be alone, John Baillie read and thought and worshipped. And through that daily, faithful discipline of will and mind and soul, it became true that the great theologian and Church statesman was first and foremost a man holy and humble of heart.

It was early in 1959 that John paid his last visit to the States, and, accompanied by his wife, carried out a Herculean programme of lecturing and preaching in the South. He was a weary man when he returned, and it soon became clear that he was seriously ill. The last year of his life was a patient struggle against pain and growing weakness, with two short periods of creative work when his indomitable will forced mind and body to the task of completing the Gifford lectures he was to have given that year. He was utterly uncomplaining, and touchingly eager to respond to any kindness and to welcome any happiness that lightened his days. Old friends ministered to him spiritually: his own loved minister, Dr. Roderick Bethune, and Bishop Warner, whom he held in very deep affection, were among them. Friends from other countries saw him for a few minutes when he was well enough to bear a visit, and one of these wrote afterwards, "Those were truly unforgettable moments. He spoke as one who is near to eternity, so that last meeting will remain a precious memory." He had hoped eagerly to take a share in the service in St. Giles' Cathedral in August to commemorate the jubilee of "Edinburgh, 1910" and when it proved impossible, it comforted him to have affectionate letters from Dr. J. H. Oldham and others to say how much his friends had missed him there. The return of his son and family on furlough from Aden brought special joy. He asked one day that his little grandson of six might have tea alone by his bedside, and he told afterwards with touching pleasure how he had lifted the child's hand to kiss it, and Peter had gently kissed his grandfather's hand in return.

But these months of illness were long and dark, and those who loved him were thankful when on 29 September the end came, and mortality was swallowed up in life. "It is hard to imagine the world and the church without him," wrote Bishop Lesslie Newbigin, "but it is a joy to think of him among the saints in heaven (what conversations he must be having!), among those who see Him face to face and await the final victory."

The letters which came to his widow after his death were most moving. Church leaders from many traditions and many lands paid tribute to what he had done for the Church and the world, and simple folk wrote simply of the help he had given to them. "What a glorious man—and many will tell you so—as a divine, a teacher, a man of vision, of prophecy, of friendship and of wit. So many here, in the U.S.A., and in the World Council, owe him so *much*. Never was a man more beloved for his good graces," wrote Archbishop Fisher. The opening sentence of the letter from Dr. Franklin Fry of the American Lutheran Church was "A hallelujah and a sigh went up all over the world at the news of Dr. Baillie's translation." In letters from Orthodox and Presbyterian, Anglican and Baptist, Lutheran and Congregational, there was not only admiration for a great leader, but love of a dear friend. And again and again there was reference to *A Diary of Private Prayer* in words such as, "Apart from the Bible itself there is no single book I use so often," or "After the death of my sister I noticed it lying on the bedside table along with her well-worn Bible."

Professor John McIntyre, who succeeded him in the Chair of Divinity, ended a public tribute with these words, "With those who were taught by him and who worked with him, the memory that remains is that of the man. Here was counsel, which clarified the issues and still left responsibility with the inquirer; a fund of humour which would shorten even the dreariest train journey; trust securely founded upon the simplicities of the Christian faith; and warmth of affection that kindled warmth."

Many on receiving the news of John's death must have turned again to his *And the Life Everlasting*. Here, as in so many of his writings, is the secret of the life of the theologian, Church statesman, and man of affairs. For the book begins with the tiny boy in the Gairloch manse answering the question, "What is the chief end of man?", and it ends with the affirmation to which his whole life bore humble and glad witness, "If we have indeed passed into the marvellous brightness of the Christian expectation, the praise is not to us, but to the Grace of God in Jesus Christ, to Whom be all praise and glory and merit throughout all ages, world without end."

ISOBEL M. FORRESTER

Edinburgh
1961

1

THE PATTERN OF HOLINESS

But as he which hath called you is holy, so be ye holy in all manner of conversation; because it is written, Be ye holy; for I am holy.

1 Peter 1. 15–16

So St. Peter writes in his letter. If you and I opened a letter that had reached us and found that in it—"Be ye holy, as God is holy"—we should probably have another look at the envelope to see whether it had come to the right address. What then is the address on this letter? It is marked quite clearly: To the strangers scattered throughout Pontus, Galatia, Cappodocia, Asia and Bithynia who had embraced the Christian faith. All these places are in Asia Minor. The Jews who lived in Asia Minor were called the Jews of the Dispersion to distinguish them from the Jews living in the Holy Land. When these Jews became Christians, they were sometimes known as Christians of the Dispersion, and to these Christians of the Dispersion—that is what is meant by "strangers scattered"—this letter is addressed. But we too who live in Scotland or in the United States, even farther away from the Holy Land, are Christians of the Dispersion in this sense, and therefore this letter is sent to our address also. Open it without hesitation, every one of you. It is meant for you.

There is nothing in it which, as the agent of the Holy Spirit of God, he is not saying to you now.

And among other things he says this: Be holy in all manner of conversation, that is in every department of your conduct, as the God who called you is holy; because it is written (in the eleventh chapter of Leviticus) "Ye shall be holy, for I am holy." Let us ask ourselves whether this is a command that we have obeyed. Can I say that I am holy? Can you say that in all your life and conduct, and in all manner of conversation, you are holy men and women? In the New Testament holy is the same word as saint. There is only one word in the Greek, which our version sometimes renders in the one way and sometimes in the other. So, if we like, we can translate St. Peter's command as "Be ye saints." But can I say that I am a saint? Can you say that you are saintly in all manner of conversation?

Not only is our answer likely to be negative, but it is also likely to be given without any very acute sense of shame and contrition. Most of us would be inclined to answer St. Peter's letter in some such strain as the following: "Dear St. Peter, I beg to acknowledge your letter written from Rome, which in the secret Christian code you call Babylon. You say you expect me to be holy. Well, I try to do my duty. I try to be honest, I try to be chaste. I try to be helpful and to do as I would be done by. I contribute to various good causes about as much of my money as I can spare. I hope I'm of some little use in the world. I go to church, I say my prayers, and I hope I can say that in some small way I am a follower of Jesus Christ. But holiness! Save the mark! I would not for a moment lay claim to anything like that. And I certainly do not pretend to be a saint. I'm just an ordinary Church member—one of the rank and file. Hoping that you will understand and

not be too disappointed, I am, my dear St. Peter, yours very
truly . . ."

Well, I'm afraid St. Peter, when he got that letter, would
be not only grievously disappointed but also thoroughly
shocked. Just as we had looked again at his letter to make
sure that it had come to the right address, so he would now
look at the signatures in our letter to make sure it had really
been written by people who profess and call themselves
Christians. For the New Testament everywhere takes it for
granted that all Christians are holy men and that all Christians are saints. Indeed the word "Christians" occurs only
three times in the New Testament, and the usual way of referring to Church members is just to call them "the saints."
When St. Paul addressed a letter to "all the saints at Colossae" or "at Ephesus" or "at Philippi," his letter was not meant
for a select few in these places, but for every one who had
been baptized in the name of the Father and of the Son and
of the Holy Ghost. And when he went on to say in his letter
to the Ephesians that God had called them to be "holy and
without blame before Him in love," he was clearly thinking
of everybody in the Church.

Now it should be said at once that neither St. Paul nor
St. Peter ever cheated himself into supposing that all Christians were without sin. Nobody could read their epistles and
think that that was what they meant. They both understood
very well that the Christian life continues to the end to be a
grim conflict with the promptings of our fallen human nature, the flesh warring against the spirit, and the spirit against
the flesh. Nor had they any greater illusions about the *corporate* life of the Christian communities in these places. St.
Paul's two letters to the congregation in Corinth, for example, show how much he knew about the sinful irregulari-

ties that were already working havoc within it. None of the churches founded by St. Paul could claim to be without blemish in its congregational life, and no single convert could lay claim to perfection in his personal life. Yet when he writes to them, he addresses them as saints and holy men. Clearly, then, a saint does not mean a perfect person, and to be holy does not mean to be entirely without sin. After which explanation you and I will perhaps be tempted to think that in that case these words do not mean anything much at all, and we shall be somewhat cheered as to our own condition.

But no! A saint or holy person does not mean one who is already perfect and without sin, but it does mean something quite definite. It means something that is perhaps even more solemn and demanding. It means one who is quite definitely *committed*. It means one who is set apart—that is the root meaning of the word—one who has consecrated himself, body, soul and spirit, to the service of the Lord Jesus Christ and has dedicated all his powers, all his interests and all his possessions to the demands of that service. That is why the phrase "holy unto the Lord" occurs so often in the Bible. Only God is holy in His own right, and for a man to be holy means that he is set apart for the service of the Holy God. "Not as though I had already attained," writes St. Paul himself to the congregation at Philippi, "either were already perfect; but I follow after . . . I count not myself to have apprehended, but . . . I press toward the mark"—toward the tape, the winning post, as we might say—"for the prize of the high calling of God in Christ Jesus." Even the great Apostle knew he had a long way to go before he reached perfection, but he was *running hard*, and he had his eye fixed, not on some half-way mark of what we profanely call ordinary rank-and-file Christianity, but on the winning-post of ultimate Christian achievement. And, as the context clearly shows, he expected every Christian in Philippi to be doing exactly the same.

That then is the question which we have to put to ourselves. Are we in this sense men and women set apart? Is this how the world is constrained to think of you and me—as holy men and women set apart for Christ with our whole lives given up to His service and every aspect of our daily conduct bearing witness to this one purpose? Do they look upon us as saints? To these same Philippians St. Paul writes: "That ye may be blameless and innocent, the sons of God in the midst of a crooked and perverse nation, among whom ye shine as lights in the world." Do we Christians so shine in the midst of this nation today? That was Christ's own phrase: "Ye are the light of the world," He said; and again, "Ye are the salt of the earth." And that is what Christ expects of every man and woman who has been baptized into the membership of His Church. He expects it of all who call themselves Christians, for nowhere in His teaching, nor anywhere in the New Testament, is the existence of any other kind of Christian recognized.

I fear the opinion most commonly held about us is that in most respects we are hardly distinguishable from our non-Christian neighbours. We are thought of as averagely decent citizens who go to church on Sundays; and I am thought of as an ordinary sort of person who happened to choose the ministry as his profession. You may say, It does not matter what people think of us: it is what we are that matters. But stop! Christ said that it was impossible to be *this* thing without all men knowing it. "A city," He said, "that is set on a hill cannot be hid . . . Let your light so shine before men, that they may see your good works, and glorify your Father which is in heaven"—and more to the same effect. It is often argued in excuse of the present inconspicuousness of our light that the whole situation has changed since New Testament times. The Christians in Philippi or Ephesus, or those "strangers scattered throughout Pontus, Galatia, Cappadocia, Asia and Bithynia," to whom St. Peter addressed his letter, were tiny bands of Christians living in the midst of a vast pagan society and known to all their neighbours as having embraced this strange new faith. They were marked men, "set apart," whether they liked it or not, from the large majority of their neighbours, often boycotted by them and already beginning to suffer persecution at their hands. Whereas now, after two thousand years of Christianity, the whole of society has been permeated by Christian influence, the public conscience of the West has been impregnated with Christian ideas, and there has been a sort of vague and diluted Christianization of all our institutions. It is accordingly argued that Christians cannot now be expected to be as "kenspeckle," as distinguishably different from their neighbours, as they were in those ancient days.

There is no doubt some truth in this, but I would put it to you that there is not very much. There has indeed been a certain Christianization of general society, but has there not been at the same time a certain secularization of our Christian life? The world has taken something of its colour from the Church, but has not the Church taken more of its colour from the world? Do you think that if Jesus Christ were to come among us again in the flesh, He would be any less a stranger in the Scotland or America of today than in Galilee long ago? Would He find Himself any more at home on our streets and in our market-places than He did in Jerusalem? Would He be less of a stumbling-block to our citizens than

He was to the Jews, or less of a foolishness than He was to the Greeks? Surely it is only a very defective historical imagination that can answer these questions with confidence. And St. Paul and St. Peter, if they were to come among us, would they be any less distinguishable, in outlook and conduct, in their interests and enthusiasms, from the generality of the men of our day than they were from those of their own? Who will dare to affirm that they would?

We may suspect, then, that the real reason why Christians are less distinguishable from the world than they used to be is not that there is more of the quality of holiness in the world, but that there is less of it in the Church. For I believe that true holiness, when by the grace of God it does appear in our midst, is as much like a light shining in the darkness as ever it was, as much like a city set on a hill that cannot be hid. There is an Indian saying that "the perfume of holiness travels even against the wind." Is it not true? When a really heroic Christian life, a life after the pattern of New Testament Christianity, makes its rare appearance among us, the fame of it still runs through all the land, and the perfume of it really does travel against all the winds of contemporary indifference and unbelief. Who shall I venture to mention as examples within our own generation—an Albert Schweitzer, an Edward Wilson, a Bonhoeffer, a Bishop Berggrav, a Martin Niemoeller, a Hugh Lister, a William Temple? Such men as these stand out hardly less clearly against the background of the modern West than they would have done against the background of ancient paganism.

But there is another test we can apply. There are many great countries in the world whose general society is still as pagan as it was in St. Paul's day, and in every one of these countries you will find sojourners of our own race who profess to call themselves Christians. What reputation have they among their pagan neighbours? Are they regarded as holy men? Do they impress the native peoples as being holy in all manner of conversation? Oh, in India and in the Mohammedan world they do know something of what holiness means. They recognize a saint when they see one. It may not be their particular brand of holiness, but they will be impressed even when they do not approve or do not understand. There are many pagans in these lands who are attempting quite heroically to live up to their own professed standards, men who are "following after" and "pressing toward the mark" with desperate resolution, however mistaken may be the direction in which they are running. And I fear the impression most of us make on them, when we do sojourn among them, is that we are less holy than they, less spiritually minded, less wholly given over to the things we are supposed to believe.

But how would it be today, if only all those Scotsmen, Englishmen and Americans who, calling themselves Christians and having been baptized in the Triune Name, have spread themselves throughout these pagan lands during the last two hundred years, had shown them what Christian holiness really means? How would it be today if, not as though they were already perfect, not as though they were anything else than fallible and sinful men, and even perhaps without much conscious attempt to evangelize or to make other men as they, they had revealed themselves from the beginning as men committed to a higher obedience, as men steadily following after—even if a long way behind—and as pressing toward the mark for the prize of their high calling in Christ Jesus?

We sometimes ask why the cause of Christian evangelism

is making such slow progress among our contemporaries both at home and abroad. We are so apt to answer the question in terms of the stony ground on which our seed is now cast, so apt to complain that we live in the midst of a hard-hearted and stiff-necked generation, altogether less responsive to spiritual appeal than were the men of former days. It might, however, be a salutary thing to give that kind of answer a bit of a rest, and to take thought rather for the defects of our own Christian witness. For the consideration that God can make use of even the most imperfect human instruments does not justify us in expecting great success for our proclamation, while we ourselves remain such colourless advertisements of the truth we proclaim.

What then is the way to greater holiness? It is a narrow way and leads through a strait gate, but we cannot with justice complain that it is difficult either to trace or to follow. Many other and harder ways have been tried. On the banks of the Ganges or on the pilgrim route to Mecca you will find men and women seeking after holiness with an unexampled concentration of purpose. They lay upon themselves heavy burdens and grievous to be born, and if such were asked of us, we might well feel daunted. But Jesus Christ says, "My yoke is easy, and my burden is light." He lays upon us no other burden than that of putting our whole trust in Him— no difficult self-immolation, no exaggerated austerities, no excesses of ascetic practice. He wants us to be kind and just and true in all the little dealings of daily life, but even that He does not expect of us in our own strength. Moreover these things are not so much the way to holiness as the fruit of it: Holiness is commitment to the service of God in Christ, but we must be careful not to understand the matter the wrong way round. It is not on the basis of our obedience that we are enrolled in Christ's service, but rather it is on the basis of our enrolment that we obey. The first thing is to be sure that we are definitely enrolled, definitely committed to Him for time and for eternity; and then perhaps we can say with St. Paul, who never hesitated to number himself among the saints, though he was humble enough to describe himself as the very least of them all: "It is no longer I who live, but Christ who lives in me; and the life I now live in the flesh I live by faith in the Son of God, who loved me and gave Himself for me."

2

WAYS OF LISTENING

Also, thou son of man, the children of thy people still are talking of thee by the walls and in the doors of the houses, and speak one to another, every one to his brother, saying, Come, I pray you, and hear what is the word that cometh forth from the Lord. And they come unto thee as the people cometh, and they sit before thee as my people, and they hear thy words, but they will not do them: for with their mouth they shew much love, but their heart goeth after covetousness. And lo, thou art unto them as a very lovely song of one that hath a pleasant voice, and can play well on an instrument; for they hear thy words, but they do them not. And when this cometh to pass, (lo, it will come,) then shall they know that a prophet hath been among them.

Ezekiel 33. 30–33

THAT passage seems difficult to understand; and so far as we do understand it, it seems remote from present-day interests. This is not surprising, because it is a Jacobean translation from a difficult ancient language, and refers to an event which took place as long ago as 9 July 586 B.C. But modern scholars can translate Hebrew much better than their Jacobean ancestors, and it is well worth while enlisting their aid to penetrate the apparent obscurity of this passage, since I believe history has sufficiently repeated itself to make the word of God which it contains very relevant indeed to our own situation in this present year of grace.

It was eleven years earlier, in the year 597 B.C. that Nebuchadnezzar, King of Babylon, successfully laid siege to the city of Jerusalem and took prisoner the eighteen-year-old King of Judah, who was called Jehoiachin and who—poor youngster—had been only three months on his throne. With the king there were carried into exile in Babylonia the queen-mother, the whole of the court, a large number of priests, the seven thousand best soldiers and the thousand best artisans and craftsmen—in fact the whole flower of the population, the whole aristocracy of birth and intellect. Yet the Babylonians did not at this time prove particularly cruel conquerors or hard masters. They did not destroy Jerusalem, but left it to manage its own reduced affairs, setting Zedekiah, an uncle of the captive king, upon the throne of Judah as a vassal prince. Nor were the captives themselves ill-treated, but were settled in a number of small self-supporting communities on the banks of the Babylonian rivers and canals.

Among the captives was a young priest of good family called Ezekiel. He was apparently at this time about twenty-five years old, and he was sent with many others to form the exile community at Tel-Abib—the original Tel-Aviv—by the river Chebar. During the first few years of his exile he was able closely to observe the life of his fellow-captives; and rumours also reached him of the life of the people who had been left at home in Jerusalem; and he grew bitterly critical of both. The people had apparently learned nothing from their bitter experience, but remained as blindly complacent as ever they had been and at the same time as heedless of the divine commands. So Ezekiel became a prophet of doom. Not indeed of ultimate doom, since he was fully persuaded that in the end, and in His own good time, God would restore the glory to Israel. But he believed that God was going to bring Israel very low indeed—to the very verge of ultimate disaster—before raising it up again. He believed that the pride of Judah must first be dragged in the dust. And especially he prophesied that the city of Jerusalem itself would be totally destroyed, and Solomon's Temple burnt to the ground. "Wherefore thus saith the Lord God, Woe to the bloody city! I myself will pile the fuel high! Heap on the wood, kindle the fire, . . . and then set the cauldron on the coals to heat, to let its copper glow, and melt out its impurity and consume its rust. Yet the thick rust will not leave it; not even the fire can purge that: Woe to the cauldron full of rust! . . . The rust is your impurity so foul. Because I would have cleansed you, and you would not be clean, you shall never be cleansed from your impurity till I glut out my fury upon you. I the Lord have said it, and I will do it, I will not refrain, I will not pity, I will not relent, I will punish you as you have lived and acted. So saith the Lord God."

Well, it turned out just as Ezekiel foretold. The vassal King at Jerusalem was so misguided as to seek the assistance of the King of Egypt against Nebuchadnezzar, but the latter had little difficulty in defeating such armies as Egypt could send against him, and Jerusalem's doom was assured. Nebuchadnezzar now knew no such word as mercy. Zedekiah the king was brutally blinded, but not before his children were butchered before his eyes, and was imprisoned for life in Babylon. Thus did the last descendant of King David who was ever to occupy the throne of Judah, perish miserably in a Babylonian dungeon. The city was looted of all its treasures, and Solomon's Temple of all its lovely gold and silver and brass-work; and then both city and temple were given to the flames. All the remaining important inhabitants were carried into exile, leaving behind them, as we read in the Second Book of Kings only "the poor of the land as vine-dressers and husbandmen." Such was the tragic event which took place on 9 July 586 B.C. "And it came to pass," Ezekiel writes in his book, "that in the twelfth year of our captivity, in the tenth month, in the fifth day of the month, one that had escaped out of Jerusalem came unto me, saying, The city has fallen."

It is hardly too much to say that when the terrible news reached the captives in Tel-Abib, Ezekiel found that he had become famous overnight. His fellow-exiles had, it is true, been already mildly intrigued by his prophecies, so that he was already a fairly well-known figure, but they had never taken him very seriously. "The vision that he seeth," they had said, "is for many days to come, and he prophesieth of times that are far off." Or they had said, "Is he not a speaker of parables?" Indeed they were so ready to discount his forebodings that, as he tells us, he had finally decided to shut himself up within his own house and to abstain from further public utterance. But now his gloomiest forebodings are suddenly justified. So the people begin to gather in little knots under the shadow of the walls and in the doorways of the houses (for in those latitudes you cannot stand talking in the middle of the street in the full glare of the sun), to discuss what they could remember of his sayings. And they also began to come about him in his own house, saying to one another, "Come and hear what word of the Lord the prophet has to pass on to us today."

But Ezekiel was not encouraged. He was not deceived. He could see that his visitors were moved as much by curiosity as by genuine concern. He had a reputation now, and the people crowded round him and listened in a way, but he could see that they were not taking his words to heart. Their hearts, he says, still "went after covetousness," that is, their thoughts were still mainly on their own petty and worldly affairs and on the pursuit of personal gain. Not even the fall of the Holy City had taught them their lesson. Jerusalem was more than five hundred miles away across the desert—a long distance in these days—and it was now more than ten years since they had seen it. So Ezekiel's solemn and terrible words were to them only "as a very lovely song of one that hath a pleasant voice, and can play well on an instrument"—as we should say, a beautiful lyric pleasantly sung and skilfully accompanied. His visitors listened attentively, but they did nothing more about it. Yet, says Ezekiel, a final hour will one day come, an hour of crisis and of judgment; and when that arrives, they will know at last that the voice of Ezekiel was the voice of God Himself seeking entrance into their hearts and lives.

And now, after that explanation, if I once more read the words of my text, but translated this time into modern rather than Jacobean English, perhaps they will seem neither obscure nor remote:

> As for you, O son of man, your fellow citizens are talking about you under the shade of the walls and in the doorways of the houses, saying to one another, Come and let us hear what is the word of the Lord today! They come to you in the usual way, they sit in front of you, they hear your words. But they will not obey them; their hearts are full of falsehood, and their minds are set upon selfish ends; so that what you say is to them like a very lovely song of one that has a pleasant voice, well accompanied on an instrument; for they hear your words, but will not obey them. Yet when the hour comes—and come it will—then they shall know that there was a prophet among them.

Now I would put it to you that that passage, far from being remote and irrelevant, is of as topical an interest in relation to our situation today as any passage could be. Our beloved country, and indeed the whole of our Christian civilization, has lately passed through the most solemn crisis in all its long history. I remember once hearing a poet say that "when Hannibal marched on Rome, Rome shook as a palm-tree shakes when a lion rubs himself against its trunk." It was a memorable phrase, which stuck in my mind, and which often recurred to me during the summer of 1940, when the fate of Europe seemed to hang upon a thread. And from that summer I remember also a wise man of God saying to me—in words that were very like the words of Ezekiel, "I believe God is going to bring this nation very low, and to humble us almost to the dust, in the hope that we may thereby be led to see the error of our ways, and repent, and return once more to His obedient service." And in those days men really did give ear to the word of God in a way that they had not done before. When our King, in consultation with our Church leaders, appointed special days of prayer for national deliverance, our churches were more crowded than I think I had ever seen them. People were remarkably ready to listen to Christian spokesmen who told them that no nation could hope to flourish that was not grounded on the worship of God and the observance of His holy laws. The idea that "righteousness exalteth a nation" gained increasing acceptance among us. The declaration that, unless we recovered hold of a Christian inheritance, the whole fabric of Western civilization was likely to collapse, was echoed from the most surprising quarters. For a little time it looked as if we might really be going to learn the lesson of our tribulation that God had in mind to teach us.

How is it now? What would Ezekiel think, if he were among us today? Would he think we had learned the lesson of Dunkirk and the Battle of Britain any better than the exiles of Tel-Abib had learned the lesson of the Fall of Jerusalem and the destruction of the Temple? And even had Ezekiel been with us in 1940, would he *then* have been as much encouraged as we were by the crowded churches, by the language of our statesmen, and by the pious phraseology of much of our propaganda? Or would he rather have said that, while we were very ready to listen to these things, and even to say them ourselves, we did not show much readiness to act accordingly? Would he have said that we listened to them only as to "a very lovely song of one that hath a pleasant voice, and can play well on an instrument?" And would he now feel that not all the bitter experiences through which we have passed, not all the retreats and all the defeats, not all the privations and all the losses, not all the exposures of our weakness and all the near visions of our doom, were enough to bring us to our senses and show us where a nation's well-being is alone to be found? And would he still be prophesying further judgment to come?

There is no doubt, I think, that there is among us today a reawakened interest in the spiritual side of life and in the question of the truth of Christianity. Men *are* gathering in knots to discuss these things in a way they were not doing ten years ago. They are gathering under the shadow of the walls and in the doorways of houses; they are writing books about them, and articles in the weekly journals. Again, during my recent visits to Germany, I was much struck by the interest displayed by large numbers of the youth in discovering what the Christian teaching really was—a knowledge which had been no part of their education under the Nazi system and which therefore had a "news value" for them which it would not otherwise have had.

All this is very heartening. It means, I believe, that men

are nearer to understanding the relevance of the Christian Gospel, and the nature of its impingement upon our human problems, than they were before the war. But the question is, *Is it going to be enough?* I mean, enough to save us from individual and social disaster. Is time going to be allowed us to solve our problems in this easy-going, academic way? Will there be time to stand and pleasantly discuss, or to sit and pleasantly listen—and meanwhile do nothing decisive about it at all? Can we still afford to say, "The vision that he seeth is for many days to come, and he prophesieth of times that are far off?"

It looks as if all these questions must be answered in the negative. It looks as if for the nations the time is very short indeed. Not more than ten years perhaps. Our wisest men tell us that unless within the next ten or at most twenty years the nations learn how to live with one another on the basis of brotherly goodwill, they are likely then to destroy one another from off the face of the earth.

And as for the individual, as for you and me personally, we may not have even that ten years, we may not have one more year, or one more month, or one more day. No single hour beyond the present is promised to me for setting my life upon a firm foundation, and finding a steadfast anchor for my immortal soul, and making my peace with God and my neighbour. This then is no hour for inconclusive academic debate either with my own soul or with another; for it may be that this night my soul shall be required of me. This is no hour in which to listen to the word and commandment of God as to "a very lovely song of one that hath a pleasant voice, and can play well on an instrument."

3

THE SPIRITUAL LIFE

But we have this treasure in earthen vessels.

2 Corinthians 4. 7

ONE THING the Bible never allows us to forget is our earthy origin. The very first thing it tells us about ourselves is that we were "formed out of the dust of the ground." That is in the second chapter of Genesis, and in the third we read also, "In the sweat of thy face shalt thou eat bread, till thou return unto the ground; for out of it wast thou taken: for dust thou art, and unto dust shalt thou return." In one of the latest Old Testament books we have Job saying the same thing: "I also am formed out of the clay." And here, in the New Testament, St. Paul reminds us of it again. "Earthen vessels," he calls us, and in another place he says that we are "of the earth, earthy." Nowadays we are perhaps more conscious of our animal than of our earthy origin. Modern man, if he is ever humble, is humbled rather by the thought of his descent from the brutes. The men of the Bible had no such idea of biological evolution or of the mutation of species. They did not think of themselves as descended from the brutes. But they *did* think of themselves as having a common origin with the brutes—an origin, as we should put it, in inorganic matter. "And out of the ground the Lord God formed every beast of the field, and every fowl of the air. . . . And the Lord God formed man out of the dust of the ground."

But the Bible also tells us that within this earthen vessel we hold a hidden treasure. Within the crock of clay there lies a precious jewel. Neither St. Paul nor any other Biblical writer thinks of this jewel as part of our natural constitution, or as anything which we hold in our own right. Rather is it something given to us, something with which we are entrusted, and which we must therefore guard and cherish above everything else in the world. What is this jewel? It is variously described. St. Paul himself describes it variously, but all his descriptions come to the same thing. Sometimes he speaks of it as the Spirit within us, sometimes as Christ within us, but here in this text he gives it a fuller description —"the light of the knowledge of the glory of God in the face of Jesus Christ." Listen to the whole passage:

> For God, who commanded the light to shine out of darkness, hath shined in our hearts, to give the light of the knowledge of the glory of God in the face of Jesus Christ. But we have this treasure in earthen vessels, that the excellency of the power may be of God, and not of us.

And above all St. Paul is conscious of the danger of losing this treasure. Sometimes he uses another metaphor, thinking of it not as a jewel, but rather as a delicate and tender flame that may very easily be extinguished. We are reminded perhaps of a famous phrase of Walter Pater's in which the two metaphors are combined, but that was a "hard, gemlike flame" that burned with a very different hue from St. Paul's. Again and again the Apostle urges us to tend this flame. "Quench not the Spirit," he says. "Wherefore I put thee in remembrance to stir up the gift of God which is in thee."

Our spiritual life is the only precious thing we possess. It is that without which all else is dust and ashes. It is that without which, in spite of all our academic knowledge, we shall become, in St. Paul's own words, as sounding brass or as a tinkling cymbal. But it is such a fragile thing and it is so easily quenched. In the bustle and hurry of the world's business you will find that it is threatened with extinction on every side. As Jesus Himself said, "the cares of this world, and the deceitfulness of riches, and the lusts of other things entering in," are always threatening to choke it. This has been the experience of men in every age, but perhaps in the modern West the danger is greater than it has ever been before. Life is more complex and more confused. Never have there been so many competing interests, so many possibilities of distraction, so many alternative ways of spending our time. Never have men had to be so carefully on their guard, in order to keep a little clear space at the centre of their lives in which the precious jewel may contrive to shine and the tender flame continue to burn.

Some of the things that threaten the spiritual life are gross and sensual sins the open acknowledgement of which would make us blush for shame. They are what the New Testament calls "fleshly lusts which war against the soul." The animal is never very far below the surface of our human nature. The nineteenth-century poet bids us "move upward, working out the beast, and let the ape and tiger die." But men can sink lower than any beast, and to call the basest human passions animal is really to slander the beasts of the field. They are not so much animal as devilish. "The impulses of nature," writes Reinhold Niebuhr, "only achieve demonic proportions when they are falsely 'mixed' with the spiritual and gain immunity from the moral censor by appropriating the moral prestige of the spiritual."

Yet we must not think that all the things that threaten the spiritual life are evil in themselves. So often it is the good that is the enemy of the best. That is why the culture of the spiritual life demands a strict discipline. You and I must be ruthless with ourselves, if the light of the knowledge of the glory of God is to survive within us. Jesus said that though "the eye is the light of the body," yet "if thy right eye offend thee, pluck it out and cast it from thee." My own experience has been that there are some enjoyments, some distractions, some ways of spending my time, from which I must firmly turn aside, if I am going to keep the Spirit alive within me. I can say nothing against them in the abstract; they may be innocent enough in themselves, they may even be all right for other people; but I know myself well enough to be sure that *I* cannot afford to indulge in them without danger of losing the Pearl of Great Price. They are like the weeds in our gardens. There is nothing wrong with the weeds in themselves. Each of them has its own humbly honourable place among our flora. But we dare not let them grow where they are, lest they choke the tender plants which the garden is intended to nurture.

And now last, we cannot be in any doubt as to the kind of spiritual discipline to which we should subject ourselves. It has all been worked out through long ages by the prophets and apostles, by the saints and martyrs. The regular practice of prayer, daily reading of Scripture, the corporate worship of God, and the reception of the Blessed Sacrament—that is the way marked out for us by the experience of the ages. There *is* no other way. Only thus can we protect the treasure which lies hidden within these earthen vessels. Only thus can we rise above the clay, and stir up the gift of God which is in us, and fan the Spirit's flame.

4

TO PRAY AND NOT TO FAINT

And he spake a parable unto them to this end, that men ought always to pray, and not to faint.

St. Luke 18. 1

THE PARABLE in question is that of the importunate widow. It represents our Lord's teaching about prayer in what many would regard as its extremest form. Nowhere in the religious literature of the world can we find stronger statements about the power and efficacy of prayer than we find in the preaching of Jesus, and this parable of the importunate widow has often been felt to be the strongest statement of all. Jesus is here telling us what we are to do when we have prayed and prayed again and our prayer has apparently not made the slightest difference to anything. And what He does is not to offer us any alternative method of obtaining our desire, but simply to say, "Go on praying all the harder, all the more importunately." To give point to this advice He asks us to think of the most unpromising human analogy we can find— the case of a poor woman without any standing or influence in the community appealing for redress to an unjust judge who "feared not God, neither regarded man." Could there be a more hopeless case? She has appealed many times, but the judge will not move a finger to help her; what more can

she do? She can do nothing, says Jesus, but appeal again—
and yet again; until at last she tires him out and he says to
himself, "I will avenge her, lest by her continual coming she
weary me," or, as may very likely be the true translation, "lest
she end by scratching my eyes out!" Could there be a
stronger statement than that of the efficacy of importunate
prayer?

St. Luke tells us that the moral of this parable is that men
ought always to pray and not to faint. The word *faint* will,
however, come to many people today as a surprise. We are so
apt to interpret the meaning of prayer as if Jesus had said that
men ought always to pray and not to *work*. That, I believe,
is precisely the mistake that most of us make in our thinking
about prayer: we think of it as an alternative to effort. We
often speak as if there were two contrasted ways of facing the
evils of our mortal lot—we may either fold our hands and
pray about them, or we may pull ourselves together and do
what we can to mend them. And standing as we do in the
tradition of what the philosophers call Western activism you
and I are almost sure to regard the latter as the nobler and
manlier way.

But it is quite plain that our Lord's way of looking at
prayer is as different from this as the day is from the night.
What He said was that men ought always to pray and not to
faint or, as the modern versions have it, not to *lose heart*.
That is to say, He regarded prayer, not as an alternative to
effort, but as an accompaniment of effort and an alternative
to despairing acquiescence and inaction. In His language, and
indeed in the language of the whole New Testament, the
opposite of praying about a thing is to do nothing about it at
all, and the opposite of working for a cause is to stop praying
about it. Prayer unaccompanied by hard work and work

unaccompanied by urgent prayer are two things that Jesus Christ not only never preached but never even contemplated as a plausible possibility. He knew well that the men who worked most tirelessly were not likely to be a different set of men from those who prayed most importunately, but the same set of men. And indeed history bears this out in the fullest possible way. It is not the philosophies of reforming zeal, but rather the philosophies of quietistic resignation, that have found no place for prayer in their schemes. Buddha, who founded the great religion of acquiescence in the East, was probably the first teacher in the world who taught his disciples that they must not pray. The Stoic teachers, who founded the great Western philosophy of acquiescence, did exactly the same. The Stoics would have been profoundly shocked by this parable of the importunate widow. Indeed all our Lord's teaching about prayer would have shocked them. To keep *asking* God for things, they would have said, means that one is not yet resigned to what His will appoints. "We should come to God without any previous desire or aversion," writes Epictetus the Stoic, "just as the wayfarer asks the man he meets which of two ways leads to where he is going, not wanting the right hand to be the way rather than the left; for he wants neither, but only that which leads him to his goal. . . . And what is best but just what pleases God? Why then do you do all you can to corrupt your judge and pervert your counsellor?" And Spinoza, the greatest modern philosopher of acquiescence, has precisely the same teaching.

Could anything be *less* like the teaching of Jesus than that? *He* had little enough hesitation, not only in making His desires known to God, but in asking and begging and importuning God to grant them. "Ask . . . seek . . . knock"

—that is His trinity of imperatives. Prayer is for Jesus not nearly so much connected with resignation as it is with *rebellion*. In that fine book with the striking title *The Faith That Rebels* the late Principal Cairns of Aberdeen points out that practically all that is said in the New Testament about prayer is said not in the interest of being reconciled to things as they are but in the interest of getting things changed.

Let us then consider one or two remarks that one hears currently made about prayer, and bring them to the test of this saying of Christ's, that "men ought always to pray, and not to faint."

Sometimes we say, "I am working so hard these days that I have no time to say my prayers." That sounds like an excellent excuse; God can hardly blame us for not seeking His presence when it is the exigencies of His own service that are keeping us away from Him. Yet I wonder whether this excuse is often very sincere. Is it really the doing of God's will that is robbing us of our hour of prayer? Would more prayer really mean less work? I have a suspicion that often it is not the quantity of work we do that makes us too tired to pray, but the amount of worry we expend on it. We moderns like to think of ourselves as terribly busy—that again is part of our so-called "activism"; and certainly we have the appearance of being busy enough. A modern city street, a modern office, a modern railway station undoubtedly give the impression of such activity as would have made our forefathers gape with astonishment. But I doubt if we are really as busy as we look—or at least if we are *doing* as much as we seem to be doing. After all a person who is too busy to pray will also be too busy to think; and what is the good of labour that is not guided by constant thought about its meaning and its end? Prayer, after all, is but thinking towards God. And I believe Jesus would have said that all deep and proper thought about our work must be directed towards God and so be of the nature of prayer. He would have said that all the good we do is done by God in us and through us. Even of Himself He said, "I can of mine own self do nothing." But there we go again, thinking of prayer as an alternative to work, whereas Jesus thought of it as an alternative to *fainting*, an alternative to *losing heart* in our labours and so failing to get anything effective done at all. I am quite sure that if only we did not set about our daily round so unthinkingly, so unprayingly; if only we gave more time to the practice of inward recollection; if only, while we are actively occupied with our tasks, we were more conscious of doing them in God's presence and by the aid of His divine grace, we would not only get more real work done, but we would do it with less expense of spirit, less weariness, less worry and less anxiety. "Men ought always to pray, and not to faint."

Take again another remark that I recently heard a man make. "If prayer is reasonable at all," he said, "it should be confined to the great spiritual issues of life. We should not pray about little things. We should not trouble God about our trifling earthly affairs." What would Jesus have to say to that? I'm sure He would have said that if anything is big enough to *worry* about, then it is not too small to *pray* about. Of course, if you are so high-minded a person that little things never worry you, then certainly there is no reason why you should worry God about them. That was exactly why the Stoics of old would not pray. They had persuaded themselves that they were, as they put it, "indifferent to all outward goods and evils." They tried to believe that nothing worried them, and nothing mattered, but the inward state of their own souls. I am afraid the poor Stoics usually bluffed themselves in this matter, but perhaps you are really the kind of man they tried so hard to be—the world's first successful Stoic. Perhaps the little things of earth never occupy your thoughts at all. There is no doubt that that is a most enviable state of mind, if you really possess it. Did not Jesus Himself bid us take no thought for such things as food and drink and clothing, and seek first the Kingdom of God and His righteousness? Ah yes, but He went on to say something else too. He said, "Your heavenly Father knoweth that ye have need of all these things." He said, "All these things shall be added unto you"—and there is a world of difference between this confidence that God will supply our needs and the Stoic's pretension that it does not matter whether our needs are supplied or not. If you never worry over the lesser things and the earthly things, then you are a remarkable exception, and very different from the rest of us—as our Lord well knew. I am afraid the common case with those who do not pray about the little things of life is that they worry about them all the more. It's not a question of whether we *ought* to worry over these things, it's a question of whether we *do* worry over them. And I'm afraid we do worry over them terribly; we lie awake at night turning them over in our minds; they spoil our peace of soul; they make us grow old before our time. Well then, says Jesus, tell your worries to God. "Your heavenly Father knoweth"—He knows, but He wants you to tell Him. He wants you to keep nothing back from Him that is in your mind at all. In prayer there must be no reserve. Surely it is a false shame that keeps you from confessing what no true shame keeps you from thinking. Surely it is a false pride that keeps you from praying about things which no true pride prevents you from worrying about. It is futile to enter God's presence pretending to be more high-minded than we really are. "Ye people, pour out your hearts before Him"—that is what Scripture says. And can one imagine anything more futile than a man praying with his *lips* to God for inward salvation of his soul, when in his heart he is all the time worrying about something quite outward and earthly—about the health of his body, or about how to make ends meet in the feeding of his family? No wonder Jesus spoke a parable unto the multitude to this end, that men ought *always* to pray, and not to faint! Or as it was put by St. Paul in writing to the Philippians: "In *nothing* be anxious; but in everything by prayer and supplication with thanks-giving let your requests be made known unto God."

Take finally another remark. "Surely," one sometimes hears it said, "it is absurd to try to change the will of God. Who are we that we should tell God what to do? If we believe in God at all, we must believe that He is already ordering all things for the best." Well, let me say first that Christian prayer is not telling God what to do; it is rather telling Him what we think we need. It is "making our requests known unto Him." In the last resort Christian prayer has always left it to God's own wisdom to decide what precisely He is to do about our need. With all his importunity the Christian never ventures to *dictate* to the Most High: he always adds, "If it be Thy will." If I thought that God were going to grant me all my prayers simply for the asking, without ever passing them under His own gracious review, without ever bringing to bear upon them His own greater wisdom, I think there would be very few prayers that I should dare to pray. Just as I believe my boy would not dare to beg things of me as importunately as he sometimes does, if he thought I was going to grant them even against my better judgment and without discrimination. He would feel, and rightly feel, that the responsibility thus thrown upon his immature judgment was far too great to be borne. "This," we read in the New Testament, "is the boldness that we have toward Him"—not that if we ask anything we like He will cause it to happen; no, but—"that, if we ask anything according to His will, He heareth us."

But there is something else to be said. You do not pray, you say, since you believe that God must know best and that therefore He is already ordering all things for the best. Well, if you believe that, then you have indeed attained—attained at least to a very lofty Stoicism, if not to quite the whole of Christian wisdom; but *do you really believe it?* You see, if you really believed that God were ordering all things for the best, then you would not only stop *praying* for things you have not got but you would also stop *wanting* them. There is neither piety nor logic in continuing to want things for which, on the ground that God knows best, you have stopped praying. Ought we, for example, to stop praying for the recovery of our friend from sickness on the ground that God knows best? Obviously we should not consider that a ground for ceasing to *work* for his recovery—to work for it by every available means which modern medicine has set at our disposal. And if it be right to work to that end, how can it be wrong to pray? Clearly we must not pray for any end towards which it is wrong to labour, but likewise we must not labour towards any end for which it is wrong to pray. There is nothing more soul-destroying than to be filled with anxious hankerings which are kept back from God. At the root of half our human tragedies lie worries that have never been resolved into prayers. "Men ought always to pray, and not to faint."

Is there some one reading this who will never be a good Stoic? Is there some one who altogether fails to face his lot with an equal mind? Are you near to fainting? Near to losing heart? Are you overborne with labour? Or worn out with worry? Or consumed with hopeless longings? Then won't you take your Lord's advice? Don't try to keep the whole thing pent up within your own heart. Share it with God. Tell Him all about it, yes, down to the last and absurdest annoying detail. "In *nothing* be anxious; but in everything by prayer and supplication with thanksgiving let your requests be made known unto God." "And he spake a parable unto them to this end, that men ought always to pray, and not to faint."

5

CHRISTIAN VIGILANCE

Watch ye, therefore: for ye know not when the master of the house cometh, at even, or at midnight, or at the cock-crowing, or in the morning: lest coming suddenly he find you sleeping. And what I say unto you I say unto all, Watch.

St. Mark 13. 35–37

THERE was no word that Jesus Christ spoke oftener to His disciples than this word *Watch*, and in this text He speaks it also to the whole world. "What I say unto you, I say unto all, Watch." It is a word that He spoke with increasing frequency, as He drew near to His death. These thirteenth and fourteenth chapters of St. Mark record the events of the two days immediately preceding His arrest, and after His arrest He had no real opportunity of extended talk with His disciples, so that these chapters really contain His final teaching. And throughout both chapters the one word *Watch* keeps recurring like the note of a drum.

If we read on through the rest of the New Testament, we shall see that this word of the Master's was like a match which set flame to the whole Christian Church during the first generation of its life. In almost every New Testament book we keep hearing the same drum note. "Watch ye, stand fast in the faith, quit ye like men, be strong," St. Paul writes to Corinth. "Continue in prayer, and watch in the same," he writes to Colossae. "Let us watch and be sober," he writes to Thessalonica. "Praying always, . . . and watching thereunto with all perseverance," he writes to Ephesus. "Watch thou in all things," he writes to Timothy. "Be watchful, and strengthen the things which remain," writes St. John the Divine, and again, "Blessed is he that watcheth, and keepeth his garments, lest he walk naked." This metaphor of keeping on one's clothes goes back, of course, to our Lord's words, "Let your loins be girt about, and your lamps burning; and ye yourselves like unto men that wait for their Lord." And the second metaphor of keeping our lamps burning, and oil in our lamps, was again given its classical expression by Him in His parable of the Wise Virgins who had trimmed their lamps and the Foolish Virgins whose lamps had gone out for lack of oil.

This teaching about watchfulness is something specifically Christian, and you will not find anything at all like it anywhere else in the literature of the world. You come nearest to it in a few places of the Old Testament, when we read of Habakkuk on his watch-tower or of the Psalmist's prayer, "Set a watch, O Lord, before my mouth; keep the door of my lips." But there is nothing like it, for instance, in the literature of ancient Greece and Rome. Vigilance is a specifically Christian grace, and it is a grace whose vitally important place in the Christian life we seldom sufficiently realize.

Now it is quite plain that this tremendous emphasis upon watchfulness in the New Testament is closely connected with our Lord's teaching about the nearness and suddenness of the end. The principal burden of His preaching, from His first sermon onwards, was that the Kingdom of God was at hand and that the time for repentance was therefore short.

He always indeed denied any knowledge of how long the time would be. "Of that day and that hour knoweth no man, no, not the angels which are in heaven, neither the Son, but the Father. Take ye heed, watch and pray, for ye know not when the time is." Nevertheless He always spoke of it as coming suddenly and soon. It was therefore not unnatural that after His disappearance from their earthly company, the disciples should have shown great impatience for this His second coming. They expected that within their own lifetimes the whole earthly order of things would come to an end and the Kingdom of God be established in all its promised glory. But it did not happen in their own lifetimes, and now some sixty more generations have passed, and nothing like what the disciples expected has happened yet. Does this mean that Christ's word *Watch* has less meaning and significance for us that it had for them?

I cannot see that it makes any difference, since it is precisely on the fact of our complete ignorance of the date of the crisis that Christ grounded His insistence on the necessity of watchfulness. "Watch therefore," He said; "for you know not what hour your Lord doth come. But know this, that if the goodman of the house had known in what watch the thief would come, he would have watched and would not have suffered his house to be broken up. Therefore be ye also ready: for in such hour as ye think not the Son of Man cometh." Nothing, then, could be more contrary to our Lord's teaching than to suppose that we may relax our vigilance because we have no reason to believe that the crisis is very near. We could afford to relax it only if we had some reason to believe that it was *not* very near. But this we never have. "And I will say unto my soul, Soul, thou hast much goods laid up for many years; take thine ease, eat, drink and be merry. But God said unto him, Thou fool, this night thy soul shall be required of thee." For you and me it may be this night. And for the Church of Jesus Christ it may be this generation.

Besides, it is most important to notice that in nearly all Christ's sayings the object towards which we are to direct our watchfulness is not His future appearing but our present state and present task. The crisis may come at any time, yet the way to prepare for it is not to be all the time on the lookout for it, but rather at each time so to attend to the work we have in hand that our Lord, when He comes, will find us doing His will. The true state of Christian readiness does not consist in being constantly keyed up to a nervous expectation, either of our own last hour or of the end of the world. It consists rather in a calm fulfilment of each duty as it comes to us; and the best preparation for the next demand that may be made on us is the punctual and conscientious fulfilment of the demand that is being made on us now. This was the very first rebuke that the disciples received after their Lord's disappearance from their midst. We read of it in the very first chapter of their *Acts:* "Ye men of Galilee, why stand ye gazing up into heaven?" And yet how many later disciples have repeated their mistake! How many sects of Christians have stood gazing up into heaven, looking impatiently for Christ's Second Coming, when they would have done better to concentrate on the humble tasks that Christ was meanwhile setting them from day to day! I remember from the years of my boyhood one woman who used literally to gaze up into heaven as she walked along the streets, being a member of some extremist sect. How foolish we boys thought her, and how foolish indeed she was to be thus nervously impatient instead of being satisfied with the knowledge that she had oil in her lamp! Christ's whole concern is that we should be ready for His final Coming, but it is *not* for His final Coming that He desires us to be directly on the watch.

What then are the things for which He desires us to be directly on the watch? I think they are three.

The first is *opportunity*. Men have always known that opportunity comes only to those who are alert for its appearance. The old word for opportunity was *occasion*, and the ancient Romans had a proverb to say that "Occasion has hair only on its forehead and is bald behind," which is the origin of our English proverb about seizing occasion by the forelock. Wait until you are well abreast of it, and then there is nothing to seize, but you will find your fingers slipping off the bald spot on the back of opportunity's head. Jesus Christ gave a new and deeper turn to this teaching of common sense. The opportunities He would have His disciples seize were not for wealth or honour but for service. These were the opportunities that He Himself was so eager to seize—not opportunities to be ministered unto but opportunities to minister. And how He seized them! And what a use He made of them! When we read of those who have rendered most distinguished service in God's world, we are apt to make excuses for ourselves and to say that so few chances have come our own way. But to read in the life of Jesus Christ is to know that, as the hymn says:

> The daily round, the common task
> Should furnish all we ought to ask.

They furnished enough for Him. What opportunities do you think Jesus Christ had that are not open to us all? His life was set in circumstances as narrow as we can well imagine. Born of peasant stock in a horse's stall, brought up in the home of a humble village carpenter, spending the whole of His short life in the remote backwater of an old-world civilization, and then cut off, almost before His prime, at the age of thirty-three: where are we to look for winds of opportunity in that story? Yet He found in it sufficient opportunity to be the Saviour of the world.

His secret was simple enough. It was that the presence of human need provided Him with all the opportunity He wanted, whereas we ask for something more. He had only to hear the sob of a bruised heart, He had only to see a human body racked with pain, or a home stricken, or a life broken, or a soul going needlessly astray, in order to be aware of the divine call to service and be quite sure that just *He* had been sent for just *that*. But you and I will often stand before human need that cries out to us with a voice loud enough to rend the heavens, and yet not be stirred by the least sense of vocation. We pass down the road from Jerusalem to Jericho with eyes raised up to heaven. If we do notice the man in the ditch, we idly wonder why he should happen to be lying there just as we were passing. *We* see only a chance encounter where Jesus heard the call of God. He sought no added sign. He waited for no heavenly voice. He found sufficient proof of the call in the presence and proximity of the need. The work itself called Him. The situation itself spoke with a sufficiently unmistakeable voice. Why then should we demand some kind of *extra* assurance that this need, which lies at our door, is there for us to mend, and that we are there to mend it? Why should we be still, like Mr. Micawber, "waiting for something to turn up"? That great physician, Sir Frederick Treves, once said this to Aberdeen students: "He who waits for a stroke of luck will probably wait till he has a stroke of apoplexy." And the same may be said of the man who is waiting for a call, when the work to be done is all the time staring him in the face.

The second thing for which Jesus Christ bids us be on the

watch is *temptation*. "Watch and pray, that ye enter not into temptation." The devil is indeed a past master in the art of the surprise attack. So subtle is he in his approach, so alluring are the forms and the dresses which he can assume, that there is little chance for us unless we are actively on the look-out for him. "Whenever I am about to commit any folly," says Bucklaw in Scott's *Bride of Lammermuir*, "he persuades me it is the most necessary, gallant, gentleman-like think on earth, and I am up to saddle-girths in the bog before I see that the ground is soft." Our only chance of escape lies in preparedness, and in the discourse of Jesus this preparedness is always connected with prayer. "Watch and pray," He repeats. And St. Paul repeats it too. "Continue in prayer, and watch in the same." Prayer is *the soul's vigil*. It is the most effective of all vigils. The devil has never such difficulty with us as when he finds us on our knees. Even then, it is true, he will not altogether own defeat. When we are praying for protection against one sin, he can make us commit another; but it is very difficult indeed for him to make us commit the very sin against which we are praying. Hence the better we understand what our besetting sins are, and the more diligently and particularly we pray for grace to overcome them, the safer we shall be. It was said that the Battle of Waterloo was really won, not on a plain in Brabant, but on the playing-fields of Eton. So it is that sin is conquered—not in the moment of temptation but in the long prayerful discipline that precedes it. And our Lord's warning is that unless we thus arm ourselves in advance, we shall find, when the temptation comes, that it is now too late. "Sleep on now, and take your rest . . . the hour is come"; what more tragic words than these have ever been spoken?

Do not let us be misled then by those who are now so ready with the opposite advice, telling us that the best way to deal with sin is never to think about it, and that it will be time enough to cross our bridges when we come to them. Rather listen to the following: "Keep the faculty of effort alive in you by a little gratuitous exercise every day. That is, be systematically ascetic or heroic in little unnecessary points, do every day or two something for no other reason than that you would rather not do it, so that when the hour of dire need draws nigh, it may find you not unnerved to stand the test." From what first-century apocalypse do you think that comes? Or from what Puritan directory? It is from William James's very modern textbook of psychology.

The third thing for which Jesus desires us to be on the watch is *truth*. For truth, no less than opportunity and security, is given only to the vigilant. "He that hath ears to hear, let him hear," said Jesus again and again. And "every one that seeketh, findeth." There are many in our day who profess complete uncertainty about the deep things of God. They complain that God has not revealed Himself to them in a sufficiently convincing way. But perhaps this complaint is no better grounded than the former complaint about lack of opportunities for service. What if it is not God who fails to speak but we who fail to listen as we ought? Was not that what Jesus meant when He said, "If they hear not Moses and the prophets, neither will they be persuaded, though one rose from the dead?" Unbelief, I know, often prides itself on its open-mindedness, yet I am persuaded that our modern unbelief is much rather due to a premature closing of our minds, and to their comfortable settlement in a narrow and restricted outlook such as prevents all further learning. I wonder if any of you have read Emile Cammaerts' recent little book *Flower of Grass*, in which he traces his own spiritual progress from complete atheism to a full and glowing Christian faith. Here is one passage from it:

> The best advice which could be given to any young man or woman would be to urge him not to allow his present beliefs, whatever they may be, to harden into prejudice; to keep an open mind, to watch eagerly what happens to him and around him, and never to close the book of life before reading the last page. There is no more fatal error than to imagine that an education is completed in school and university. We should always be at school, we should always prepare for some examination, till the final examination. A secular life tends to narrow our outlook because it induces us to close the book after reading the first chapter. A Christian life compels us to leave the book open to the end.

That is much more like Habakkuk who said, "I will stand upon my watch, and set me upon the tower, and will watch to see what he will say unto me"; or like Samuel who said "Speak, Lord, for thy servant heareth."

> O give me Samuel's ear,
>   The open ear, O Lord,
> Alive and quick to hear
>   Each whisper of Thy word,—
> Like him to answer at Thy call
> And to obey Thee first of all.

During the long black-out evenings of our war-time winters I found myself re-reading a great many of the books that were written about the First World War. In one of these books the question is asked as to what kind of man it was who really won the war for us, and the answer proposed is this: "He was a plain man awake all night in a ditch." Is not that the kind of man who by the grace of God will always win the battle of life—a plain man on the watch?

6

ONE THING IS NEEDFUL

Now it came to pass, as they went, that he entered into a certain village: and a certain woman named Martha received him into her house. And she had a sister called Mary, which also sat at Jesus' feet, and heard his word. But Martha was cumbered about much serving, and came to him, and said, Lord, dost thou not care that my sister hath left me to serve alone? bid her therefore that she help me. And Jesus answered and said unto her, Martha, Martha, thou art careful and troubled about many things; But one thing is needful: and Mary hath chosen that good part, which shall not be taken away from her.

St. Luke 10. 38–42

TOLD as it is with that admirable brevity which is the despair of us long-winded moderns, that is one of the most famous stories in the world. It is famous because it presents the ultimate human problem in the homeliest possible guise. A few half-bantering words spoken at an Eastern dinner-party, but they touch the very quick of our human situation and go to the root of all our philosophics! It was a great occasion for that little household in the unnamed village when Jesus came to a meal. Martha, the householder, very naturally wanted to make it something of a festival. She "was cumbered about much serving," that is, she had prepared a great variety of dishes. But Mary, her younger sister,

61

only "sat at Jesus' feet and heard his word." It was therefore
not unnatural that Martha should feel a little aggrieved and
say, "Lord, dost thou not care that my sister hath left me to
serve alone? bid her therefore that she help me." It is the
Lord's answer that has made the incident so famous: "Martha,
Martha, thou art careful and troubled about many things:
But one thing is needful, and Mary hath chosen that good
part, which shall not be taken away from her."

That is how the answer stands in the Authorized Version.
It appears in a variety of different forms in our earliest
manuscripts of the Gospels; but one reading which appears
in several of the best manuscripts would be translated as
follows: "Martha, Martha, you are worrying and bustling
about many dishes. But few dishes are necessary, or indeed
only one. And Mary has chosen that best dish from which
she must not be drawn away." There is in that a double
meaning and a fine play upon words. Jesus begins by saying
that a simple meal is all that is required and that Martha
need not have troubled to prepare so many dishes. And then
he breaks off into seriousness and says, "After all; only one
dish is necessary—the best dish of all, the dish which Mary
chooses when she sits at my feet and hears my word."

I am afraid it cannot be denied that our own lives are for
the most part like the life of Martha. We are worried and
bustled about many things. We have a multitude of cares,
we have a multitude of interests, and we go from one thing
to another, sometimes feverishly, sometimes in a desultory
way, according to our temperament. Many of us have household cares just as Martha had; these days, indeed, there are
few of us who have not some household cares. We are
"cumbered about much serving," and often have more things
to do in a day than the day will easily hold. But even if we

have no household cares, no dishes to prepare and no dishes to wash, our lives still incline to the same confused pattern. There are as many Marthas in the university as there are in the home. Students are cumbered with the study of many subjects, and too often they form a kind of unrelated jumble in our minds. Some of them we fancy to be indigestible (and perhaps Mary thought the same about some of Martha's concoctions), but in any case we have not sufficient time and capacity to do justice to them all. And when we leave the cloisters of learning to go out into what we think of as the great world, things are not going to be any easier, but even more difficult; and life is going to be more complicated still. If it was so in our Lord's day, how much more in our own! How much more complex a thing has the life of the average citizen become during these two thousand years! What a jumble our modern life is! Macbeth's phrase describes it even better than he knew—a fitful fever.

> After life's fitful fever he sleeps well.

Or even that other and extremer phrase of his:

> a tale
> Told by an idiot, full of sound and fury,
> Signifying nothing.

Or I might quote the words of the hero in a recent American novel: "I feel like I had enough Chaos in me for the Lord to create another world out of."

And now into the midst of this chaos, into the midst of the fitful fever, into the midst of the jumble, comes the clear word of Christ: "But one thing is needful." *Porro unum est necessarium*, as our forefathers knew it by heart from the Vulgate Latin version. And I believe that deep down within us we always knew this to be true. We knew that the reality of life did not lie in that chaos of concern but in something entirely simple and entirely single. Throughout all the multitude of our occupations and interests we were somehow aware that life must have a single meaning, that only one thing really mattered, and that, if only we could find it, there was no more than one pearl of great price.

This does not mean that we can evade the complexity of life by simply contracting out of it. That, I am sure, would be to misunderstand our Lord's advice. His words to Martha were very gently spoken. He knew well that dishes must be served, though perhaps not quite so many or so sumptuous. He knew that there must be cooking and washing and cleaning and mending, that the house must be swept and garnished, and that the bustling life of the village must still go forward in market-place, workshop and field. Only a very humourless reader of the story could understand Him to mean that we should all sit all day in rapt contemplation as Mary was sitting then. There is a sense in which the complexity of life is of the very essence of our human situation, and part of our opportunity as well as of our burden. I think even St. Paul tends to underestimate this necessary complexity in one passage in his First Epistle to the Corinthians, though he is careful to forewarn us that here he is giving us only his own private opinion and not any relevation he has received from the Lord. Let me read the passage in Dr. Moffatt's modern translation:

> I have no orders from the Lord for unmarried people, but I will give you the opinion of one whom you can trust, after all the Lord's mercy to him. . . . Are you tied to a wife? Never try to untie the knot. Are you free? Never try to get married. . . .

> The unmarried man is anxious about the Lord's af-
> fairs, how best to satisfy the Lord; the married man
> is anxious about worldly affairs, how best to satisfy
> his wife—so he is torn in two directions. The un-
> married woman or the maid is also anxious about the
> Lord's affairs, how to be consecrated, body and
> spirit; once married, she is anxious about worldly
> affairs, how best to satisfy her husband. I am saying
> this in your own interests, not that I want to restrict
> your freedom.

Well, the old bachelor! Coming from the great Apostle,
the opinion is indeed not one which we can lightly disregard;
but he claims no higher authority for it, and in any case I
am sure it would be a mistake to interpret the story of Martha
and Mary in the light of his words.

There was nothing corresponding to a university in the
Holy Land in our Lord's time, and the particular variety of
interests and concerns that fills the lives of modern students
was then largely unknown. But after all, the principle is the
same, whether it be household or political economy that
occupies us, whether we are busy with our bodies or only
with our minds. In the last resort only one thing is needful,
and yet you and I must study many things and we have a
rightful interest in many things. It may be that some of us
confuse ourselves with too great a variety of interests, and
study too many subjects, as Martha prepared too many dishes;
but the real source of our confusion lies rather in the fact that
we study them too much out of relation to the one thing
that will give ultimate meaning to them all. The way to give
unity to the complexity is not hastily to contract out of the
complexity, though that also may have to be done in part, but
to discover how the complexity itself can be made to sub-
serve the *unum necessarium,* in which alone is our peace and

by which alone we shall all be judged, and even judge ourselves, in the end.

What then is the *unum necessarium?* What is the one thing
needful, the good part which Mary chose? I think we all
know a number of things which it is not. We know that it
does not consist in any kind of material gain or riches, since a
man may gain the whole world and lose his own soul. We
know also that it does not consist in making for ourselves a
successful career in the world. How many outwardly successful careers there are that have a cancer at their core! Even of
many *useful* careers the same is true; there are men whose
work is of great service to society, but who are themselves no
ornament to it; men who have done the right thing but who
are themselves all wrong. So also I have in my library certain
books with which I could ill afford to dispense, while the
personal history of the writer is best forgotten; they are the
right kind of books, but he was the wrong sort of man. In
such cases a man's work may take on an impersonal form and
contribute usefully to the general good, so long as it can be
detached from the living personality of the man himself. But
if all hearts were open, and all desires known, how different it
would be! I fear there are not a few so-called benefactors of
the human race who would be found to be doing us more
harm than good, if only we could see with the eyes of God!
You remember St. Paul: "lest that when I have preached to
others, I myself might be a castaway."

The one thing needful, then, is not money or power or
fame or a successful career. And again, I think we know quite
well that it is not what we call culture—a cultivated mind.
Perhaps the most horrid product of our universities is the
superior kind of intellectual, the man who thinks he has found
the pearl of great price because he has developed certain

learned interests. This particular way of evading the final issue is one that has been very much with us ever since the Renaissance. It has been the temptation of Renaissance man to make a religion of his humanism, turning means into ends, and absorbing himself completely in antiquarian or linguistic or scientific study or in some form of art for art's sake. And yet we know it to be as true of the humanist, the grammarian, the scientist and the aesthete as it is of the man of business and affairs, that the very intensity of his absorption in these departmental interests may be in part only a cover for the uncertainty that still haunts him at the core of his being. For knowledge after all is a very different thing from wisdom, and it is only wisdom that matters in the end.

I think, then, we are fully prepared for the discovery that the one thing needful is the same for us all—the same for peasant and plutocrat, the same for household drudge and highbrow student, and (incidentally) the same also for students and professors. What is the good part which Mary chose? The story puts it quite simply: she "sat at Jesus' feet, and heard his word."

And that is what it is. I suppose the psychologists would want to express it by saying the one thing needful is that we should be perfectly adjusted to the total situation in which we find ourselves. I suppose the philosophers would say the one thing needful is that we should have come to terms with reality. Both statements are, if properly understood, true. What is wrong with most of us is that at the centre of our beings, behind all our apparent success and our absorption in life's varied interests, there is a hidden maladjustment and a flight from reality. But the final reality, and the ultimate fact of our total situation, to which we need to be adjusted, is God. That indeed would be my definition of

God: God is He with whom we have ultimately to do, the final reality to which we have to face up, and with whom we have in the last resort to reckon. But for you and me to face up to God is to face up to Jesus Christ. It is in Christ we see what God is like and what He requires of us. It was the coming of Christ that placed men before the ultimate decision. Oh, there may be all sorts of unanswered questions in our minds about the nature of His coming, and about the nature of Him who came, but we know well enough that He challenges us to a decision; and that ever since He came nearly two thousand years ago, our civilization has had such an uneasy conscience as it never had before.

To sit at Jesus' feet and hear His word—that is the *unum necessarium*. Not, of course, to sit there idly and to hear with an otiose and curious interest, as men had heard the words of Scribes. The word of Jesus is not a word that can easily be listened to in that way. It is such that we have either to stop our ears to it or else make it the master word of all our hearing. I am quite sure this is the one thing that matters for us all. It is far from being the only thing permitted to anybody, but it is the only thing necessary for everybody. It was a favourite contention of that great man, Baron von Hügel, that only by renouncing the claim to be *everything* could religion maintain its claim to be the *chief thing*. But it is the chief thing not only in the sense that it is the best of things, but in the sense that it alone is necessary, that without it all other good things are as dust and ashes, and that they must every one, if need should arise, be surrendered for its sake.

Once long ago on the North-West frontier of India a troop of robbers came upon a man leading a fine horse richly caprisoned. "O brother, who art thou?" they asked. "I am So-and-So, the servant of Such-an-One," he replied, "and I am taking this horse to my master's son as a gift from his uncle." Then they seized and carried off the horse, and beat the man, but let him go.

Later in the day, he fell in with another troop of robbers who likewise asked him who he was. "I am So-and-So, the servant of Such-an-One," he replied, "and I carry to my master's son as a gift from his father a gold chain which is concealed within my turban." They found the chain, and took it and most of his clothes, but let him go.

At last he reached his destination, and presented himself to his master's son; who, seeing a limping footsore man wearing only a raggard loincloth, asked him in astonishment who he was. "I am So-and-So, the servant of Such-an-One, who is your father," he replied, "and I bring to my master's son this gift."

And so saying he took from his armpit the great pearl, now called the Mountain of Milk, which to this day is chiefest among the treasures of the Amirs of that land.

So let us, if need be, surrender all other things, but hold to the one thing needful against that day, when we shall present it at last to the Son of God, to whom now with the Father and the Holy Ghost be all glory and praise. Amen.

7

THE YOKE

Come unto me, all ye that labour and are heavy laden, and I will give you rest. Take my yoke upon you, and learn of me; for I am meek and lowly in heart: and ye shall find rest unto your souls. For my yoke is easy, and my burden is light.
St. Matthew 11. 28–30

WE SHOULD prefer perhaps to be under no yoke of any sort and to have done with burdens altogether. We should prefer to live entirely untrammelled lives, and to do our thinking apart from all restraints. Why should man, who is lord of all the creatures, not be lord also of his own life? Why should he subject himself to any discipline at all, whether in thought or in action? Jean Jacques Rousseau began a famous treatise with the sentence, "Man was born free, but he is everywhere in chains"; and his advice to us was that we should rid ourselves without delay of every yoke and chain that had ever been forged, including of course the yoke and chain of Christ. Those who can bring themselves to read his *Confessions* will have some idea of the result. The fact is that human life quickly disintegrates, as the life of Rousseau disintegrated, if it refuses to submit itself to some kind of yoke. Man is in his very nature a dependent being. He was made to serve some end greater than himself, and to contribute to a glory greater than his own. His centre is not in himself, and if he tries to find his centre in himself, he is on the sure road to corruption. For this reason he must, if his humanity is to survive, serve some master and subject himself to some sort of discipline. Now discipline is just the Latin word for learning; and to subject oneself to the Christian discipline is just to take seriously Christ's words, "Take my yoke upon you, and learn of me." When a man submitted himself to the instruction of any teacher, he was said among the Jews to take that teacher's yoke upon him. Discipleship and discipline are two slightly different words for the same thing.

Christ is quite frank, then, in warning us that to follow Him means to submit ourselves to a certain yoke and to bear a certain burden. He warns us that to be His disciples involves a restriction upon our liberty. To be a Christian is to accept a particular frame of reference within which all our action, and also all our thought, is to be carried on. We are now under authority and no longer free to do as we please. There are certain limits which we must not transgress. There are certain actions from which we must abstain, there are thoughts which we must not think, and even certain fields into which our imaginations must not wander. We must, as St. Paul told the Corinthians, "cast down imaginations, and every high thing that exalteth itself against the knowledge of God," and bring "into captivity every thought to the obedience of Christ."

Our Lord, then, does not claim that His disciples bear no yoke upon their shoulders but only that theirs is the easiest of yokes and the lightest of burdens. Perhaps after all it is not possible for man to be entirely without a yoke and burden. The freedom which men think to gain by eschewing all discipline is a false and illusory freedom, for in this way they merely become slaves to their own fancies, their own appe-

tites, their own ambitions. To be one's own master is in fact
to be the meanest of slaves. The free-thinker tries to plumb
the infinite by discarding the Christian frame of reference,
and all other frames of reference such as might restrict the
free play of his thought; but what he succeeds in doing is
only to confine his thinking within strictly human and ter-
restrial limits; for the free-thinker is usually a humanist and
as often as not a materialist. No man was ever more proud
than was Rousseau of having won complete freedom for himself, but what one feels as one reads his *Confessions* is that
with every chapter he is forging another link in the chain that
ultimately strangled his intelligence no less than it had already strangled his virtue.

When men discover the illusoriness of an undisciplined
freedom, they are likely to seize the first yoke that comes to
hand; and the heavier it is, the readier they are to wear it.
That is what has lately happened in so many parts of Europe.
An earlier generation was wont to exult in having achieved
complete freedom for itself; but the very taste of this hard-
won freedom seems to have turned sour in the mouth of the
present generation. In the youth of one country after another
we have witnessed the returning desire for submission. They
no longer want to carry each his own burden. They no longer
want to go each his own way. They eagerly desire somebody
to lead them. They want to be told what to do, what to say,
and even what to think. Thus they have fallen victims to the
worst kind of leadership and to the blindest of blind guides.
Such has been the fate of our enemies, but that is not to say
that the same danger did not also menace us in our own land.
A few years before the Second World War Sir Michael
Sadler, the doyen among our educational authorities, thus de-

scribed the prevailing attitude among Oxford undergraduates: "The young are eager and hungry—for faith, for work, for a leader whom they can trust and follow without question. . . . They are not interested in what at one time I would have gone to the stake for—I mean liberty of thought. Give them the possibility of ardour in achievement and they would not care a hang about—for example—the freedom of the Press. . . . Once the young have found their leader and accepted his purpose, there will be a revolution. That, one suspects, is the mood of tomorrow."

Well, let us hope that the danger of false leadership has to some extent been averted in this country. Let us hope that the returning desire to find a definite pattern of life will lead our youth back to the acceptance of the Christian pattern rather than tempt them to experiment with the patterns of the modern secular systems. Let us hope that the sight of peoples under the political yoke of oppressive régimes will lead men to realize how easy and light, by comparison, are the yoke and burden of Christ.

But why is it that Christ's yoke is easier and His burden lighter than all others? He gives us the reason when He says, "For I am meek and lowly in heart." There is no doubt that here lay the most obvious difference between Christ and the Scribes and Pharisees who loved "the uppermost room at feasts and the chief seats in the synagogues" and concerning whom Christ said also that "they bind heavy burdens and grievous to be borne, and lay them on men's shoulders, but they themselves will not move them with one of their fingers." There is equally little doubt that here lies the obvious difference between the bearing of Christ and that of His principal rivals in our own day. Could there be a more striking contrast than that between the meek and lowly Christ and the corrupt pattern of leadership displayed by your strutting dictators, your Napoleons and Hitlers and Mussolinis?

But yet we ask, what is the precise connection between Christ's meekness and the easiness of the yoke which He asks men to bear? Why should it be less burdensome to follow a pattern of humility than a pattern of pride? And how can we thus find rest unto our souls? It is because humility is the obverse side of confidence in God, whereas pride is the obverse side of confidence in self. The very essence of the Christian pattern of life is that we rely for our salvation wholly upon God and not at all upon ourselves. Christ's yoke falls easily upon our shoulders, because He Himself has borne it for us, and His burden weighs lightly because He has taken the weight of it upon Himself. "They themselves will not move them with one of their fingers," He said of the Scribes and Pharisees; but Christ bore our griefs and carried our sorrows; the chastisement of our peace was upon Him; and so we have found rest and peace unto our souls.

And we have also found the only true freedom—"the liberty wherewith Christ has made you free." The man whose will acknowledges no master thinks himself free, but he is not really so, because he has to bear all his own burdens, and these are too much for him. But if we are humble enough to become Christ's bondsmen, He gives us back our freedom by bearing all our burdens for us.

> I was not ever thus, nor prayed that Thou
>   Shouldst lead me on;
> I loved to choose and see my path, but now
>   Lead Thou me on.

8

USE AND WONT

Make straight paths for your feet.

Hebrews 12. 13

Not forsaking the assembling of ourselves together, as the habit of some is.

Hebrews 10. 25

And he came to Nazareth, where he had been brought up: and, as his custom was, he went into the synagogue on the sabbath day.

St. Luke 4. 16

RECENTLY 1 was walking to church with my five-year-old grandson when we met a little girl coming in the opposite direction. My grandson asked her, "Aren't you going to church?" and when she said "No," he replied with what I thought was a mixture of pride and gentle reproof, "I always go to church on Sunday mornings."

The trivial incident set me thinking about the value and disvalue of custom in the spiritual life. There have always been some high-minded people who set no store by it at all. What is the good, they have asked, of worshipping God by habit, of confessing our sins to Him by habit, of saying our morning and evening prayers by habit, of saying grace before meals by habit? It is, they say, only on those occasions when we are stirred by a deeply felt need of such actions that we

75

should perform them at all, and they quite naturally refuse
to believe that all who, for instance, go to church every
Sunday morning, are regularly visited by such a sense of
need just as the clock approaches the hour of eleven. As we
know, the churches in the United States of America are now
very crowded—so crowded that very many of them have to
have repeat services every Sunday morning; identical services
with the same sermon, the same hymns, the same prayers.
There are many, chiefly outside America, but also some
within it, who are very scornful of this development. A
friend of mine, a distinguished Anglican churchman, spoke of
it in an article written after his return from a visit as "the
horrible religiosity of the United States." When I myself was
in America recently, newspaper reporters used often to ask
me, "Dr. Baillie, do you think there is a revival of religion in
this country?" Well, I used to answer that I thought that was
too exalted a name to give to what was happening, that I did
not think these crowds were going to church from the very
highest motives, but neither did I think that their motives
were altogether unworthy. Many of them go, I believe, out
of a certain sense of insecurity. They are acutely conscious of
the challenge now being presented to the Western democ-
racies by the communist half of the world. The communists
know what they believe. They are all united in the same
fanatical conviction. And this, as it seems to me, has led
our American cousins to ask themselves whether the traditional American way of life, to which they so rightly cling,
can continue to prosper if it should cease to be supported by
an equally fervent faith of its own. But what other faith could
this be but the Christian? Our Western culture has always
been centred in the Christian tradition. That has been its
spiritual rallying-point, and the question is whether our

familiar way of life, our cherished home life and our standards of public morality, can hope to continue under their
own momentum, if this rallying-point is lost to them. I believe many American parents, who had themselves received
a Christian upbringing but who had long ceased to subject
themselves to any Christian discipline, now tremble to think
what may happen to their own children, if they are allowed
to grow up in complete detachment from the church and
without any such Christian instruction as they themselves had
received. So they are returning to the church in astonishingly
large numbers and bringing their children with them. No
doubt something of the same sort may be happening in Great
Britain, but it is from the United States that I have chosen
my example.

I say, then, that this is not the worst reason for going to
church, but that it is certainly not the best. For it is more
than doubtful whether a habit of pious observance can really
sustain itself for very long unless it finds some much deeper
nourishment than this. No mere habit can long endure that
is not constantly invigorated and refreshed by a fervent faith.
What has kept the Christian tradition alive through all these
long centuries is that among the many who joined in the
worship of God because it was the prevailing custom, there
were always some in every age and in every place who joined
in it from a profound sense of their own need of God and
who found in Him their only abiding joy. These were they
who could say with the Psalmist, "I was glad when they said
unto me, Let us go into the house of the Lord"; "As the
hart panteth after the water-brooks, so panteth my soul after
thee, O God. My soul thirsteth for God, the living God:
when shall I appear before God?"

Nevertheless—and it is of this that I want particularly to

speak—there is a place for custom, for the formation of habits, and for doing things by use and wont, even within the life of the most spiritual-minded. For there is not one of us who remains on the same level of spiritual-mindedness all the time. The hart does not always pant for the water-brooks. The soul does not always thirst for the living God. Even the greatest saints have complained of what they called periods of spiritual *dryness*, periods of darkness and doubt, when the spirit seemed to die within them; and the great mystics have testified that they all had to pass through what they called "the Dark Night of the soul." And that is why it is the most saintly of men who have been foremost in submitting themselves to a rigid discipline of Christian observance, forming regular habits from which they never allowed themselves to deviate. They have followed the advice of the Epistle to the Hebrews in the first of my texts, "Make straight paths for your feet"; which is as much as to say "Make rules for yourself and stick to them." On days when the spiritual flame burns brightly within us, so that there is nothing we so much desire as communion with God, we have perhaps no need of a rule. But it is just then that we should lay down our rules. This is the time for surveying, for taking our bearings and shaping our course; so that, when desire begins to fail and the spiritual flame burns low, the discipline to which we have committed ourselves will still keep us in the right way and in the middle of the road. You know Matthew Arnold's verse:

We cannot kindle when we will
    The fire that in the heart resides.
The spirit bloweth and is still.
    In mystery the soul abides.
        But tasks in hours of insight will'd
        Can be through hours of gloom fulfill'd.

Do not let us be deterred by any false pride from having to do many things merely from use and wont. There is much room in the lives of us all for a rigid discipline to which we shall adhere even in our driest hours and on our most listless days. It has always seemed to me a great protection to have some things in our lives that are the same every day—and every week. It protects us against self-deception, self-indulgence, but also and chiefly against an unhealthy self-absorption. You see, if I have no rule, if I have marked out no straight paths for my feet, I shall continually be saying to my self: "I don't feel like going to church today" or "I don't feel like saying my prayers this morning"; and so I shall not say my prayers and I shall not go to church. Oh, how much attention the men of the present generation pay to their own precious feelings! We are so introverted, so much preoccupied with our own states of mind. Yet some of us are beginning to see the weakness of a religious practice that invites us to consult our feelings before lifting up our hearts to God and making haste to do His will. For *is it* not when I don't feel like prayer that I am more in need of the help it can give? Is it not when I don't feel like joining the congregation of God's people that I most need their fellowship to take me out of myself? And perhaps it is just when I don't feel like partaking of the Blessed Sacrament that I most need to have my feelings transformed by feeding upon Christ's body and blood. Shall we not then take this sacred author's advice? On our days of clear vision and keen desire—and God knows they are few enough!—shall we not mark out straight paths for our feet and then, on our listless days and our dry days, keep steadfastly to these paths, and walk between the fences of them, if God so help us by His grace?

It is particularly with the matter of regular church-going

that my second and third texts are concerned. In one of them the same author, the writer of the Epistle to the Hebrews, says: "Let us consider one another, to provoke unto love and to good works: not forsaking the assembling of ourselves together, as the habit of some is." The Authorized Version says "the manner of some," but the Greek word is *ethos*, which rather means habit or custom. So that even in that first century of the existence of the Christian Church, there were some who had formed the habit of merely occasional attendance. But notice also how the sacred author implies that we are to join in the assembly of the saints *both* for our own sakes *and* for the sake of our fellow Christians. We are to stir up one another to love and to service. For Christianity is in its very essence a corporate affair. You can't really be a Christian all by yourself. You cannot retire into your own shell or into your own corner and live the Christian life there. A single individual cannot be a Christian in his singleness. He can be a Christian only in his togetherness with his fellows. It is when at least two or three are gathered together in His name that Christ promised to be there in their midst. Not long ago I read the autobiography of Dorothy, Duchess of Wellington, published under the title of *Far Have I Travelled*, and came upon this passage: "My grandfather lived to be very old. . . . Though he was the most religious of men, he never entered a church in his life, but went through the whole service"—it would be the Church of England Order of Morning Prayer—"on his knees alone in his study." But what a poor and truncated version of the Christian religion that after all was! It is recorded that on one occasion a similar remark was made by a leading citizen of Chicago to the famous evangelist D. L. Moody who was visiting him in his own drawing-room. "I do not see," said the man, "that I cannot be just as good a Christian outside the church as within it." Moody said nothing but stepped to the brightly burning fire and, picking up a blazing coal in the tongs, allowed it to burn by itself. In silence the two men watched it smoulder and go out. "I see," said the other, and next Sunday he went to church.

And now look at my third text, in which St. Luke records our Lord's own practice in this matter. "And he came to Nazareth, where he had been brought up: and, as his custom was, he went into the synagogue on the sabbath day . . ." You might have thought that custom had no place in our Lord's life, but here it is, "As his custom was." You might have thought He had no need to go to church, yet in this also He identified Himself with His human brethren. He went to the synagogue every sabbath day. This, of course, was the Jewish synagogue, for it was not until Pentecost that the Christians began to meet in a separate place of their own. But the word synagogue simply means "place of assembly," and when the Epistle to the Hebrews says "not forsaking the assembling of ourselves together," it is this word that is used for "assembling"—*episynagōgein*.

Surely, then, if our Lord Himself made straight paths for His feet, we are called upon to do the same. If He had His own rules for Himself, we should not be above having rules for ourselves. If He submitted Himself to a regular spiritual discipline, His followers should do not less. If He had His fixed customs, surely we should have ours. For in this too He has left us an example that we should follow in His steps. And still He comes to church with us every sabbath day. He is present always, and it is to meet with Him that most of us come. Let us then not forsake the assembling of ourselves together, as the custom of some is, but let us follow His better custom: and let us make it our rule, with Coleridge's Ancient Mariner:

> To walk together to the kirk
> With a goodly company.
> To walk together to the kirk
> And all together pray,
> While each to his great Father bends,
> Old men, and babes, and loving friends,
> And youths and maidens gay.

9

HIS IMMEMORIAL PLAN

Behold, I stand at the door, and knock: if any man hear my voice, and open the door, I will come in to him, and will sup with him, and he with me.

Revelation 3. 20

EVENING in Asia Minor; a street in a prosperous commercial city; a patient figure standing outside one of the dwelling-houses and knocking at the door; and within, the lamp-lit interior, a table set with bread and wine, whilst nearby reclines the householder taking no apparent heed of the summons. Why is this simple picture, painted in the quietest domestic style, one of the most famous pictures in the world? It is because, of all the pictures that have ever been painted or imagined, this is the one that most perfectly symbolizes how things are between Christ and the human soul.

Look with me then at each part of this picture separately. And first let us look at the figure who is outside. You and I cannot be in any doubt who He is. We have been familiar with that waiting Presence ever since we can remember. We have been hearing that knock as far back as we can remember hearing anything. It is mingled with our earliest memories, and at the very hour of our birth it sounded in the house where we were born. For not only has Christ been standing at your heart's door and mine all our lives through, but He has been standing at Europe's door for almost two thousand years; so that you and I were born into the long heritage of that knocking. It is quite impossible to read through even an ordinary text-book of European history without being aware of the difference Christ's presence has made to every page. The story of Europe is simply the story of how it has behaved in face of Christ's challenge; it is that far more essentially, far more truly, far more deeply, than it is anything else.

Notice where the figure is standing. He is outside on the doorstep, and the door is shut. I fear that that part of the picture is only too true. That is where Christ spends most of His time—outside the door. All these long weary centuries He has been standing out there. I think that that is just the impression we have, as we read the story of Europe—the impression of Someone just beyond the threshold, Someone not quite in the story but, as it were, haunting the margins of the page. European history shows us a marvellous succession of lamp-lit interiors, in Constantinople and Rome, in Milan and Moscow and Madrid, in Versailles and Westminster and Holyroodhouse. Our Lord is never far away from any of those, but it is only into a very few that He has actually been admitted. His usual place, alas, is just outside the door!

Consider next the quality of the knock—as it is heard from inside the room. It has in it a strange union of patience and persistency. At one moment you will be impressed by its unobtrusiveness, at the next by its ceaseless repetition. Apparently the waiting figure never goes away, yet never makes the least attempt to force an entrance. The latch itself does not move: He does not lift the latch—that must be done from within; He only knocks, and knocks, and knocks. Can't you hear the knocking now?—I mean at the door of *your own* heart, and *now*, just in this moment? Is there not a summons of which you are even now aware? Is there not something seeking admission into your heart? I cannot tell you just what form it takes; only you know that. Perhaps it is some particular task that is calling you—some opportunity of service which has been waiting at your door for years but to which you have never yet responded. Or perhaps the knocking that disturbs you this morning is associated with some shameful thing you have done, some hard word you spoke at the breakfast table this morning, some poisoned arrow of an unkind look, some mean advantage you have taken of somebody, some unchastity, some little piece of dishonesty—or perhaps some *big* piece of dishonesty? I cannot tell just what it is that is knocking at your heart's door, but I know that whatever it is, it is Christ. For Christ comes to us in all sort of disguises. Indeed He never comes to us *except* in some disguise. There is a picture I often see on people's walls which represents to us Christ appearing in all the glory of His passion among the London crowd on the steps of St. Paul's, and underneath is the legend, "Is it nothing to you, all ye that pass by?" But it is an incongruous picture. You may indeed see Christ standing on the steps of St. Paul's, but it will always be in some incognito—in the likeness, it may be, of a beggar or a stranger or a little child.

> I come in the little things,
> Saith the Lord:
> My starry wings
> I do forsake,
> Love's highway of humility to take:
> Meekly I fit my stature to your need,
> In beggar's part
> About your gates I shall not cease to plead—

As man to speak with man—
Till by such art
I shall achieve my Immemorial Plan,
Pass the low lintel of the human heart.

It is the artifice He uses always. Christ will never come to
you as you see Him in the paintings. He came to His first
disciples in the likeness of a Galilean peasant, but even that
was a disguise assumed by Him who was the Son of God. To
the lintel of your heart He comes in some other disguise. He
is there now. Something is knocking at your heart's door.
Something is seeking entrance. It is Christ; and you know it
is Christ.

Now look at the man inside, the Laodicean householder.
He hears the knock. You can tell that from his behaviour.
And yet he takes no notice of it; he *tries* to behave as if he
did not hear it. For one thing, he has now been hearing it for
so long that often, for long periods, it hardly penetrates his
consciousness at all. As time has gone on, he has become increasingly successful in persuading himself that there is nothing there to hear. He can eat now without its disturbing his
digestion. He can even sleep through the knocking at night.
It has almost, by this time, become part of the general hum
of the city's life. Sometimes he tells himself that that is all
it is—the roar of distant traffic, as the caravans from Tiflis
and Trebizond unload their corded bales in the market-place.
It is only a cart-wheel rattling over the noisy cobbles. Or
perhaps it is but the wind rattling the shutters as it howls and
whistles down the Lycus valley. He tells himself these things,
but he does not really believe them. Deep down inside him
he does not believe them. You can tell from his behaviour
that his self-deceit has only half succeeded. He affects un-
concern but he is not really at ease. There is a nervous haste

about the way he eats his bread. And though he sleeps, it is not very soundly or peacefully, and the knocking enters into his dreams. Yes, there is no doubt of it—he hears the knock and he knows what it is. He knows he is wanted. And he knows who it is who wants him. He knows that He who is standing on his doorstep is none other than Jesus Christ the Son of God.

And *you* know that too. You know that this knocking at your heart's door is Christ soliciting an entrance. Often you have tried to shut your ears to it. Or when you could not do that, you have told yourself tales about it, trying to explain it away. But you have had little comfort from the pretence, and little peace of mind. I think the challenge that Christ has brought to human life is hardly less strikingly manifested in those lives that have refused Him than in those that have accepted Him. Those chapters of European history from which Christ has been excluded bear hardly less remarkable witness to His power than those in which He has been admitted to the feast. The lesson European history has to teach us is that Christ may be accepted or rejected, but He cannot be ignored. Nothing in that story is quite as it would have been if Christ had never lived and never died. You and I cannot really rob Christ of His sovereignty. There is a sense, as the theologians have always insisted, in which nothing we do can either add to His glory or diminish it. If we accept Him, we shall but share in the glory that is already His; but if we reject Him, our lives will still bear their own sad witness to a glory that they can never share. As St. Anselm said long ago, "He who flees from under the will that commands does but rush under the will that punishes." The house at whose door the King of Glory has once knocked can never be the same house again.

But now look at the next bit of our text: "If any man hear my voice, and open the door. . . ." Notice the force of that *if*. It means that Christ never forces an entrance into any house. It means that Christ never invades any man's heart against that man's will. He waits always until the latch is lifted from within. That is man's part in religion. That is what you and I are expected to do—to lift the latch. Christ will do all the rest Himself. And yet—and yet—has not Christ something to do even with the lifting of the latch? If after many days the Laodicean finds at last that he can stand that knocking no longer, if his resistance is at last worn down, so that he yields and opens the door, then who is it that has really opened it, the Laodicean or the stranger? You may say, of course it is the Laodicean. And you are right; it *is* the Laodicean. And you say, it was he himself who decided at last to do it; and again you are right: the decision was most certainly his. Aye, but what *made* him decide? I am sure he himself would be the first to tell you that it was the knock. "I did not *want* to open the door," he would say to you. "I wanted very much to keep it shut. But I just could not hold out any longer against that continual knocking, so I *had* to go and let the stranger in." That is the account of the matter that has always been given by those who have most gloriously let Christ into their hearts and lives. They have insisted that while indeed the latch was never forced by Christ but lifted by their own hand and of their own free will, yet behind that motion of their hand and behind that decision of their will there was the irresistibility of Christ's appeal. They have insisted that in the last resort they could not help themselves. They have said, "The love of Christ constraineth us." That is the doctrine of prevenient and irresistible grace.

And now the last bit of our text: "If any man hear my

voice, and open the door, I will come in to him, and will sup with him, and he with me." What a change now comes over the whole scene! A moment ago the atmosphere was one of strange discomfort, with always that undercurrent of strain and strife. But now there is only joy and communion and a glorious, happy feast.

That too is a perfect symbol of Christ's dealings with the human soul. Religion always appears under two contrasted guises, corresponding to these two contrasted scenes. It is first an austere and disturbing challenge, and then it is a glorious and happy feast. Under the first of these guises religion is known to us all. In every man's life that first scene has been enacted. We all know what is meant by that stranger on the doorstep, and by that annoyingly persistent knocking, and by the terrible strain it puts on the man within. So much of religion is familiar to everybody. But the tragedy is that many a man's acquaintance with religion stops at that point, and he knows nothing of the second scene, when Christ is inside the room. That is why so many people carry with them all through their lives the idea of religion as a harsh and joyless thing, a thing that limits their freedom and cramps their spirits and makes them unhappy. That is why so many writers of books present religion as a morbid perversion of the human spirit. That is why so many of our novelists portray religious folk as peevish and morose killjoys with long, sour faces and a melancholy and dyspeptic disposition. They are familiar only with the first scene, when Christ is outside the door; and of that scene every one of these things is true and not a whit exaggerated. It is quite true that when religion is known to men only as an unanswered summons, it can be the cause of more misery and melancholy and dyspepsia, more morbid introversion and more nervous disorder, than anything else in the world. Some men have just enough religion to make them desperately miserable. All some men know of religion is hell.

But some of us know religion under a quite different guise. Some of us are familiar with the second scene. We know the situation in which Christ is inside the room. And so instead of associating religion with fear and constraint and gloom and nervous depression, we always associate it rather with freedom and peace and joy. The other day a friend of mine, who was reading by my fireside, flung down his novel impatiently and exclaimed, "I often think that many of these modern novelists can never have met a really good man." And I do think some of them must be very sorely puzzled to understand why the New Testament should always connect religion with things like joy and gladness and liberty and peace of mind. For there is only one way by which a man can come to know anything of Christ's peace, and that is by responding to His challenge. He will never know Christ's companionship until he has yielded to His claim. He can know nothing of religion as communion until he has first known it as an answered summons. The glories of religion must always be hidden from those who evade its demands.

> Solid joys and lasting treasure
> None but Zion's children know.

And then lastly, notice only this. Notice how, when once the latch is lifted, Christ takes charge of all that follows.

> Christ shall the banquet spread
> With his own royal hand.

Lately He stood outside on the doorstep, waiting for you and me to do something—to let Him in; but now that we have let Him in, He seems to do everything else Himself. He takes complete charge of every detail of the feast. He who was lately a claimant is now a giver. He who was lately a beggar is now more host than guest. "I will come in to him," He says, "and will sup with him, and he with me." O what a grand banquet it is! O what a master of ceremonies! O what sweet communion! O what happy fellowship! O what lack of constraint! O what liberty! O what joy!

10

NIGHT THOUGHTS

When I remember thee upon my bed, and meditate on thee in the night watches.

Psalm 63. 6

At midnight I will rise to give thanks unto thee because of thy righteous judgments.

Psalm 119. 62

Mine eyes prevent the night watches, that I might meditate in thy word.

Psalm 119. 148

THE MEN who wrote these words lived about two thousand and five hundred years ago. They lived in a small and obscure Eastern land that was backward in the arts of civilization, even according to the standards then prevailing in several other parts of the world. They were shaggy tribesmen with long hair and flowing beards. They walked over their stony, scrubby soil either with bare feet or shod only in sandals, and clad in a loin-cloth, a tunic and a home-spun blanket. They ate with their fingers from a common dish, pouring their wine from goat-skins into clay cups; and though they were careful to rinse their fingers before setting to, in other respects they fell far short of our modern Western standards of cleanliness. Even today when we visit those lands of the Near East, and move among their descendants or among other Semitic tribesmen who are their near relations, we find ourselves regarding them as immeasurably inferior to ourselves who have all the apparatus of civilization at our command—knives and forks, bathrooms, well-built houses, well-made furniture, well-tailored clothes, railway trains, motor cars, and all the rest of it.

Moreover, the men who wrote these words *knew* hardly anything as we account knowledge. They had never been to school, for there were no schools in that simple ancient land. They knew nothing of science. In mathematics they had not reached the *pons asinorum*. They thought the earth was flat, and when the sun set, they thought it was taking a bath in the Western seas. If you had asked them to draw a map of the world, they would have shown you a sort of oval, reaching westwards half way across the Mediterranean, eastwards only as far as Persia, northwards only to the Balkans, and southwards no further than to Arabia and Abyssinia. Their medical knowledge was confined to the use of a few herbs and simples. They could speak no word of any language save their own rough mother tongue. They had no books except the papyrus rolls in the synagogues. They had little taste for art. They were full of superstitions, for they believed in witches and incantations and spells and evil spirits. To us who are the heirs of all the intervening ages, standing in the foremost files of time, they appear as homespun as the clothes they wore, the simple-minded children of a rude and artless race.

We find it difficult, perhaps, to put ourselves in the place of such men and to imagine what the inside of their minds would be like. Sometimes, when a P. and O. liner calls at Jeddah or Aden or some such place, we catch a glimpse of Semitic tribesmen dressed very much as these must have been, and still living very much the same sort of life—for time moves very slowly on the fringes of the Arabian sands. It is only a fleeting glimpse we get, and in order to understand what manner of men they are, we would like to see the inside of their houses, but especially to know what is going on inside their heads. When *we* lie browsing on our deck chairs on the liner, we have such a wealth of things to think about, our minds being richly stored with the heritage of the centuries. And in bed at night, before sleep overtakes us, or when sleep deserts us, what a profusion of thoughts compete with each other in our minds, what a kaleidoscope of images crowd in upon us, reflecting all the complexities of our daily life! But what would these primitives have to think about as they lay on their wicker-work of palm leaves, wrapped in their oriental rugs?

Fortunately we know the answer, for they have told us very plainly. And here it is: "When I remember thee upon my bed, and meditate on thee in the night watches." "At midnight I will rise to give thanks unto thee, because of thy righteous judgments." "I prevented the dawning of the morning, and cried: I hoped in thy word. Mine eyes prevent the night watches, that I might meditate in thy word."

Can we read these words without a sudden sense of humiliation and a collapse of our self-esteem? Where is now our vaunted superiority, our proud boast of belonging to a higher culture? We are not so stupid as to think that our real selves are identical with the front we show to the world, or that the words we speak in public are a true reflection of the kind of men we are. We knew well that, as the emperor Marcus Aurelius once set down in his private note-book, "The soul is dyed the colour of its leisure thought." Modern psychology has convinced us of that, even when we had refused to learn it from any other quarter. If a psychologist wants to understand the sort of man I am, he will not listen to the conversation I make, or read what I write on paper; he will rather try to penetrate beneath this official selfhood to my most secret thoughts. He is not interested in the public show-places of my mind, but in its hidden nooks and crannies. He would like to know what visions I see in the clouds of my tobacco smoke as I lie back in my easy chair. He would like to know what I think of as I lie awake in bed, and he will question me in particular about the dreams that come to me when at last I drop off to sleep. It is the inner life that counts. When, therefore, I compare myself with these unkempt old worthies who wrote the Psalms several thousand years ago, when I try to measure my real worth and my real wisdom and enlightenment against theirs, I can find no truer standard of comparison than in honestly answering the question they have already answered for themselves: What do I remember on my bed, and on what do I meditate in the night watches?

Very often, I fear, our thoughts upon our beds are definitely harmful, or definitely shameful. They are such as we would not let other people know for all the world. Sometimes we are offered a penny for our thoughts, but a thousand gold guineas would not buy these thoughts from us. We allow our imagination to wander, or even we deliberately guide it, down forbidden alleys where we would hate men to know that we had ever loitered. Or again, we take this opportunity to nurse our grievances, to think hard thoughts about those who have wronged us and perhaps to plan petty revenges upon them; or to build for ourselves avaricious castles in the air. But even when our thoughts are not thus dishonourable, they are often far from being exalted or sublime. They may not always be mean and base, but they are usually—oh, so trivial! They fasten on molehills and make them seem like mountains. They flutter over the superficialities of life, and seldom reach more than a little way down to its true heart and centre.

But these old worthies went to the centre at once. When they laid their heads upon their rude pillows, they remembered God. When they composed themselves to sleep, they were thinking upon His word. And if they woke up in the middle of the night, it was to meditate on His precepts and to give thanks to Him because of His righteous judgments. The Hebrews divided the night into four watches, and in many circumstances these had to be literal watches, with somebody awake and on guard. This was the case when they slept in tents in the wilderness, but it was also the case in the Temple of Jerusalem, where some of the Levites had to be on duty as watchmen and Temple attendants during every part of the night. I think some of these Psalmists were dwellers in tents—perhaps in the course of a pilgrimage to Jerusalem, and others were Levites on night-duty at the Temple; and what they are telling us here is how they spent these hours of enforced wakefulness.

Which of us then, do you think, can boast of having the richer and more significant life—we with our civilized manners, our wide acquaintance with the world, our many-sided education, our vast accumulation of heterogeneous knowledge, our immense variety of interests, but without any deep spiritual life to give unity and singleness of meaning to it all; or they with their primitive habits and barbarian manners, their simple rules of thumb in place of science, their minds as scantily furnished as their houses, their large areas of complete ignorance, but all the time living very close to the centre of things, living the hidden life of the spirit and—even in the watches of the night—meditating upon God?

Surely there can only be one answer. There is a sentence of Reinhold Niebuhr's that has stuck in my mind: "The modern urban man, shuttling between his office and his apartment, is hardly as significant a person as a traditional peasant in his village community." And I remember another sentence from the pen of a Spanish writer: "The life of a nun in a bare cell is more genuinely intense and active than that of a New York business man." And yet I do not want to live in a bare cell. I do not want to live the life of a nun, or of a traditional peasant, or the life that the Hebrew Psalmist had to live. If we are wise we shall not need to choose between his blessings and ours, for in themselves these are not mutually exclusive. We do not need to go back to eating with our fingers in order to enjoy his blessings, or to go about the streets in a loin-cloth and home-spun blanket. We can meditate on God's word between clean sheets quite as well as wrapped in an oriental rug that had not been washed since it was woven. We can have a deep spiritual life without surrendering the advantages of a more advanced civilization, without exchanging our reaping-machines for sickles, and our watches for hour-glasses, and our electric light for a rush stuck in a saucer of oil. And as for all our modern knowledge —our scientific understanding of the world we live in, the treasures of European literature, the glories of European art —these are all good gifts from God, meant for the enrichment rather than the impoverishment of our spiritual life, giving us not less but rather much greater ground for singing His praises and for rising from our beds to give thanks to His Holy Name.

Our fault is not, then, that we accept God's gifts but that, in accepting them, we forget the Giver. And what that means in practice is that we remain on the surface of life and never reach down to its vitalizing centre. It means also that our life becomes a jumble of conflicting interests and concerns, with no grand simple pattern to it such as would make everything fall into its rightful place. Our modern lives have enough and to spare of diversity in them, but they are sadly lacking in unity. The Psalmists' lives would seem to us lacking in diversity, but about their unity there was no doubt. And whenever they had a little time to spare, they used it to strengthen that unity. In their own oft-repeated phrase, they made certain that, however mind and body were occupied, their "heart was fixed." Or if they had no time to spare during the day, they got up at midnight, or rose in the morning a little earlier than they had to—just to think about God.

Yet we do the Psalmists grave injustice if we suppose that they had to hold themselves down to this practice of inward recollection as to a hard and unwelcome task. To feel like that about our times of devotion is to show that we are still held captive by the circumferential things, and that our hearts are not really fixed to the centre. I remember how rebuked I once felt by hearing a saintly contemporary of my own declare how precious to him were the few hours he could snatch from his busy life for the enjoyment of quiet times with God, and how reluctantly he at last rose from his knees, when duty called him elsewhere. That is how we ought to feel. That is how the Psalmists felt. "My soul shall be satisfied with marrow and fatness; and my mouth shall praise thee with joyful lips; when I remember thee upon my bed." "How sweet are thy words unto my taste! yea sweeter than honey to my mouth!" "As the hart panteth for the water-brooks, so panteth my soul after thee, O God." And that is how they felt too about going to worship God in His holy temple—in sad contrast to those of ourselves who drag weary feet to church as a matter of unwilling duty. "I was glad when they said unto me, Let us go unto the house of the Lord." "My soul longeth, yea, even fainteth for the courts of the Lord: my heart and my flesh crieth out for the living God."

Our conclusion then must be that while indeed our modern life is adorned with many gifts and graces which the Psalmists lacked, we remain vastly their inferiors until and unless we bring these greater blessings into the same intimate relation to the true heart and centre of things as they brought their more restricted ones. In the last resort that is the only thing that matters. Only this one thing is absolutely needful. Here is only this one pearl of great price. And though there are a multitude of other things now available to us that are good and beautiful in their time and in their appointed place, they are all as froth and bubble, if we are without this one thing. Therefore, O my soul, think thou upon God! O mine eyes, prevent ye the night watches that I may meditate in His word!

11

THE THEOLOGY OF SLEEP

Except the Lord build the house, they labour in vain that build it: except the Lord keep the city, the watchman waketh but in vain. It is vain for you to rise up early, to sit up late, to eat the bread of sorrows: for so he giveth his beloved sleep.

Psalm 127. 1–2

MY SUBJECT is the theology of sleep. It is an unusual subject, but I make no apology for it. I think we hear too few sermons about sleep. After all, we spend a very large share of our lives sleeping. I suppose that on an average I've slept for eight hours out of every twenty-four during the whole of my life, and that means that I've slept for well over twenty years. What an old Rip van Winkle I am! But then, what Rip van Winkles all of us are, or will one day become! Don't we agree then that the Christian gospel should have something to say about the sleeping third of our lives as well as about the waking two-thirds of it? I believe it has something to say, and that this text from the hundred and twenty-seventh psalm serves as a good beginning for the exposition of it.

The point the Psalmist is making is that we should not carry our cares and anxieties to bed with us. Beds were made for sleeping, not for worrying. He takes two examples. If a man is building a house for himself, how likely he is to carry the care of it to bed with him, anxiously going over the details of it in his mind and counting up all the things that may be going wrong! Or again, how often men have lain awake for fear of danger! That would no doubt be more common in the Psalmist's day than in our own. The cities of Judaea were not as well policed as Edinburgh or Glasgow or New York, nor were the frontiers of Judaea so well guarded against external enemies as those of our own land today. And yet I suppose there are some who are kept from sleep even now by the thought of burglars, or perhaps of fire. But the Psalmist is only giving examples, and we can think of many others. Do not many citizens of today carry their business worries to bed with them? Do not housewives carry their household worries—perhaps worries as to how to make ends meet, or as to how one pair of hands can do all the things that ought to be done on the morrow? And how well I know that many students carry their examination worries to bed with them—to the great detriment of the scripts they write! Well, what the Psalmist says to all such is that they are forgetting God. They are forgetting that, when they are asleep, God is wide awake. They are forgetting what another Psalmist had already taught them, that "The Lord is thy keeper," and "He that keepeth Israel shall neither slumber nor sleep." What man can do towards the success of his plans is very little. "Man proposes, but God disposes." What you and I can do for the security of those dear to us is equally little, if God is not caring for them. "Except the Lord build the house, they labour in vain that build it: except the Lord keep the city, the watchman waketh but in vain." Therefore "it is vain for you to rise up early, to sit up late, to eat the bread of sorrow: for so he giveth his beloved sleep." During the bombing of London, a woman was heard to excuse herself for having stayed quietly in bed, by saying "Well, I reflected that God does not sleep, and there seemed no reason why *both* of us should stay awake."

1. Sleep is surely one of God's most precious gifts, as none know better than those who are victims of insomnia. It has been ordained that our lives here below should consist in an alternation of activity and rest, of sleeping and waking; but we could not support the activity if we had no rest, or the waking hours if we had no sleep. How blessed a thing it is, then, that we are not expected to retain the conscious control of our lives by night as well as by day, but that we are allowed to lay the reins in God's hands, entrusting ourselves to His care when we are least able to care for ourselves. But we must really *entrust* ourselves. Sleep comes best to those who most put their trust in God. That is what the Psalmist means by saying, "He giveth his *beloved* sleep." His beloved are those who trust Him. There is no better soporific than a trustful heart, no surer way of having a good night's rest than to commend ourselves to God's keeping, in believing prayer, before we go to sleep. Of course some men and women are constitutionally light sleepers. Insomnia may be due to any one of several different causes. But if the commonest cause of it is a mind unrelaxed from care, its best cure is to cast all our cares upon the Keeper of Israel who neither slumbers nor sleeps. Elizabeth Barrett Browning is not much read nowadays, but perhaps no poem of hers is better remembered than the one that begins with the verse:

> Of all the thoughts of God that are
> Borne inward unto souls afar,
> Along the Psalmist's music deep,
> Now tell me if that any is,
> For gift or grace, surpassing this—
> 'He giveth His beloved, sleep'

2. But now, if instead of following the Authorized Version, we consult the margin of the Revised Version, we shall find this different rendering: "He giveth unto his beloved *in* sleep." And that is the rendering accepted by most of the commentators. It also embodies the richer thought, for it speaks not only of the blessedness of sleep itself but of the blessed things that are given us through its agency. When we sleep we are not merely being released, we are also being restored. Without any effort of our own a new supply of energy is being built up within us. We wake with fresh vigour, and we look out on the world with different eyes. Our minds are clearer, and very often we find that the problems of the day before have settled themselves while we slept. "Settled themselves," we say. The Psalmist would rather have said that God had settled them for us. My teacher, Hugh Mackintosh, used to quote a saying of George Macdonald's: "Sleep is God's contrivance for giving man the help He cannot get into him when he is awake." During the day we are so anxious to keep the reins of our destiny so entirely in our own hands that God has to wait until we are asleep in order to do for us and in us those things which we cannot do for ourselves. Some of the saints have gone so far as to say that among the things God gives to His beloved in sleep is an increase in their love of Him. They have claimed that their growth in grace has not been confined to their waking hours. In that beautiful little book *The Practice of the Presence of God* you will read how Brother Lawrence, the seventeenth-century monk of Lorraine, used to say that "Those whose spirits are stirred by the breath of the Holy Spirit of God go forwards even in sleep." They wake up better men than they went to bed! If we find this difficult to believe, is it not only because we habitually suppose ourselves to be much more the masters of our spiritual develop-

ment than we actually are? If some of the processes that are necessary for our physical well-being go on more advantageously in sleep than in waking life, because the will then relaxes its too despotic control, why should not the same be true of some of the processes that advance our spiritual well-being? Do you remember Wordsworth's lines?

> Nor less I deem that there are Powers
> Which of themselves our minds impress;
> That we can feel this mind of ours
> In a wise passiveness.

> Think you, 'mid all this mighty sum
> Of things for ever speaking,
> That nothing of itself will come,
> But we must still be seeking?

Or consider this quaint stanza in one of Isaac Watts' hymns which we do not usually sing:

> God is my portion and my joy,
>   His counsels are my light;
> He gives me sweet advice by day
> And gentle hints by night.

I want to read to you also the prayer which the great Dr. Arnold of Rugby School, Matthew Arnold's father, used to repeat every morning before beginning his day's work in the school:

> O Lord, we have a busy world around us. Eye, ear and thought will be needed for all our work to be done in the world. Now ere we again enter into it, we would commit eye, ear, and thought to Thee. Do Thou bless them and keep their work Thine, that as through Thy natural laws our hearts beat and our blood flows without any thought of ours for them, so our spiritual life may hold on its course at those times when our minds cannot consciously turn

to Thee to commit each particular thought to Thy
service, through Jesus Christ our Lord. Amen.

That is a good prayer to say when we get up in the morning,
but I would put it to you whether there is not one very like
it which it is good to say when we lie down at night.

3. I cannot, however, leave the subject of the theology of
sleep without saying something about the theology of dreams.
Some indeed say they never dream, and if that is true of you,
you will naturally not be so much interested in this last
heading. But dreams have played a large part in religious
history. All through the ages men have believed that God
visited them in dreams—ever since Jacob's dream at Bethel,
from which he woke up saying to himself, "Surely the Lord
is in this place." And do you remember Mercy's dream in
The Pilgrim's Progress? Let me remind you of it. Her mother
Christiana asked her one morning, "What was the matter
that you did laugh in your sleep to-night? I suppose you were
in a dream." To which Mercy replied thus:

> 'I was a dreamed that I sat all alone in a solitary
> place, and was bemoaning of the hardness of my
> heart. Now I had not sat there long, but methought
> many were gathered about me to see me, and to hear
> what it was that I said. So they hearkened, and I went
> on bemoaning the hardness of my heart. At this some
> of them laughed at me, some called me fool, and
> some began to thrust me about. With that, methought
> I looked up and saw one coming with wings towards
> me. So he came directly to me and said, Mercy, what
> aileth thee? Now when he had heard me make my
> complaint, he said Peace be to thee; he also wiped
> mine eyes with his handkerchief, and clad me in
> silver and gold. He put a chain about my neck, and
> ear-rings in my ears, and a beautiful crown upon my
> head. Then he took me by the hand and said, Mercy,
> come after me. So he went up, and I followed till

we came at a golden gate. Then he knocked, and when they within had opened, the man went in and I followed him up to a throne, upon which One sat; and He said to me, Welcome, daughter . . . so I awoke from my dream. But did I laugh?'

'Laugh!' replied Christiana. 'Ay, and well you might to see yourself so well. For you must give me leave to tell you that I believe it was a good dream; and that as you have begun to find the first part true, so you shall find the second at last. God speaks once, yea twice, yet man perceiveth it not; in a dream, in a vision of the night, when deep sleep falleth upon men, in slumberings upon the bed. We need not, when a-bed, lie awake to talk with God; He can visit us while we sleep, and cause us then to hear His voice. Our heart oft-times wakes when we sleep, and God can speak to that, either by words, by proverbs, by signs and similitudes, as well as if one was awake.'

'Well,' said Mercy, 'I am glad of my dream; for I hope ere long to see it fulfilled, to the making of me laugh again.'

Of course, the great change that has overtaken the theology of sleep is that the ancients believed dreams to be premonitory of the unborn future, whereas we moderns regard them rather as uprisings from the half-buried past. But this difference of interpretations does not at all affect Christiana's main contention that God can be with us even in our dreams. We are too apt to think that our dreams come to us by mere chance, that there is no rhyme or reason about them; yet such a notion is quite as much opposed by the modern Freudians as by the ancient soothsayers. Again, we think that we have no control over our dreams, and it is indeed true that we have no direct control over them—we cannot, as we lie awake, decide what we are going to dream about after we go to sleep. Nevertheless we can be certain that the power which controls our dreams is the same power that controls our life as a whole. If we have surrendered our hearts to God in the sunlight, He will be with us no less during the hours of darkness. Nor can the Devil get at us by night, if we have not allowed him *some* entry by day. It is certain that if there were no evil in our waking souls, there would be no evil in our dreams. But, of course, evil is always at our doors, at least in the form of temptation. Even the greatest saints have never got rid of that. So long as we remain in the flesh, suggestions of evil will continue to appear on the thresholds of our minds and imaginations. Nor should we allow that to trouble us unduly—so long as we do our best, by God's help, to refuse them any effective harbour. And if that is true of our waking life, how much more likely is it to be true of our dreams, when sleep relaxes the will, when what the Freudians call the Censor or the Super-Ego is no longer on guard! If, therefore, our dreams are sometimes unsavoury, we should not let that worry us overmuch. We should not brood over them, but rather laugh at them. They are of the Devil, and that wonderful Englishwoman of the fourteenth century, Lady Julian of Norwich, tells us how she always used to laugh at the Devil, refusing to take his caperings seriously. And yet—and yet—there is after all one way in which we can exercise some control over our dreams, and that is by the proper direction of our thoughts before we retire. All experience goes to show that the quality of our night's rest depends in large measure on the frame of mind in which we go to bed and compose ourselves to sleep. I shall conclude by saying this—and it is something of which I have continually to keep reminding myself: Every man who calls himself a Christian should go to sleep thinking about the love of God as it has visited us in the Person of His Son, Jesus Christ our Lord.

12

WHEN I AWAKE

As for me, I will behold thy face in righteousness: I shall be satisfied, when I awake, with thy likeness.

Psalm 17. 15

SOME of the Psalmists are sorely troubled by the fact that wicked men so often seem to prosper; but this Psalmist, while noting the fact, is roused to no envy by it. He believes his own lot to be incomparably better. In the preceding verse he speaks of "men of the world, which have their portion in this life"; but as for himself, he says, he will behold God's face in righteousness, and be satisfied with His likeness.

But what does "when I awake" mean? Awake from what? It is not altogether easy to say.

1. Some of the commentators believe it to mean, "when I rouse myself from brooding over what these prosperous wicked men have done to me." That certainly appears a possible interpretation. There is nothing that "gets us down" like the feeling that we have been unfairly dealt with. It is very difficult to know oneself the victim of injustice and not to be embittered by the knowledge. The commoner thing is that the knowledge rankles and festers within us until it becomes grossly exaggerated and we develop, if not exactly a sense of persecution, at least something of what might be called a hard-luck complex. When unprincipled men appear to flourish through their very lack of principle, while we ourselves remain so scrupulous and self-effacing that nothing ever comes our way; or even when, let us say, some other members of the household seem consistently selfish and "get

away with it" every time, while our own efforts to be un-
selfish are coolly taken advantage of; then resentment mixed
with envy and jealousy threatens to creep over our minds
like a black cloud, and we can no longer see things in their
true colours or proportions. Perhaps that had happened to
this Psalmist; and perhaps when he says "when I awake," he
means "when I shake myself free of this dark obscuring cloud
of envy and jealousy." When this happens, so that he sees
things again in the full daylight of a just valuation, then his
envy vanishes like a bad dream of the night. He is more than
satisfied with his own portion. If he has really been true to
principle, if he has really served his fellows unselfishly, if he
has really been all the time on the Lord's side— but not forgetting the force of that "if"—then he has chosen the better
part and there is no room for repining.

Nobody reads Emerson nowadays, and I do not greatly
blame them, but there is a passage in his essay on Compensation that is worth recalling. He tells us how shocked he
was by having lately heard a sermon to the effect that the
good are miserable in this life and the wicked happy, but
that a compensation will be made to both parties in the next
life. What did the preacher mean? he asks.

> Was it that houses and lands, offices, wine, horses,
> dress, luxury, are had by unprincipled men, whilst
> the saints are poor and despised; and that a com-
> pensation is to be made to these last hereafter by
> giving them the like gratification hereafter—bank-
> stock and doubloons, venison and champagne? That
> must be the compensation intended: for what else?
> Is it that they are to have leave to pray and praise?
> to love and serve men? Why, that they can do now.
> . . . The blindness of the preacher consisted in de-
> ferring to the base estimate of the market of what
> constitutes a manly success, instead of confronting
> and convicting the world from the truth.

You remember how another Psalmist says, "Whom have I in heaven but thee? and there is none upon earth that I desire beside thee." Perhaps then it was to this same realization that the writer of this seventeenth psalm awoke, when he said, "As for me, I will behold thy face in righteousness; I shall be satisfied, when I awake, with thy likeness."

2. Other commentators, however, think the waking referred to is just the ordinary waking up from a night's sleep at the beginning of each new day; and they refer as a parallel to the eighteenth verse of Psalm 139: "When I awake, I am still with thee"—which obviously refers to waking up in the morning.

A certain little girl was once asked by her solicitous parent, when she woke up in the morning, "How are you feeling this morning, dear?" To which she answered, "I don't know; I haven't *tried* yet." The little girl, you see, wanted a moment or two in which, as it were, to take a sounding. I believe most of us take such a sounding every morning when we wake out of deep sleep. Very often memory returns to us with a rush— we remember the state of our fortunes as they stood when we went to sleep, and the prospects for the new day now before us. Sometimes, therefore, the return of consciousness is painful, while at other times it is a delight. I well remember how when I was young our circle was broken by a sudden death, and how I was afraid to go to sleep that night, fearing lest the sudden remembrance of it when I woke in the morning would mean that the first bitterness of realization would have to be experienced all over again. On the other hand, we can imagine a young girl waking up on the morning after being asked in marriage by the one and only right man, and thrilling to the joy of it a second time. And then perhaps to know that it would be the same every morning afterwards!

—so that she could say with confidence about the man of her choice: "I shall be satisfied, when I awake, with his likeness."

Perhaps that is just what the Psalmist is here saying to God. And what a wonderful thing it is to say! It is a good rule that our last thought at night and our first thought in the morning should be about God; and yet for the true Christian it is much more than a rule: it is his natural impulse. Indeed one of the Psalmists tells us that he is in the habit of getting up sooner than would otherwise be necessary, just in order to think about God. "I prevented (i.e., was in advance of) the dawning of the morning . . . that I might meditate on thy word." If I have really pledged myself to God's service in life and in death, the situation so created will naturally reinstate itself in my consciousness every time I wake from sleep. Every morning it all comes back to me. Every morning I remember afresh whose I am and whom I serve. Well, am I satisfied with Him? Am I satisfied with His likeness?

His likeness? But do we know what He is like—this God to whose service the Christian is committed? Yes we do indeed: *He is like Jesus.* That is how the New Testament always speaks of Jesus—in the Epistle to the Hebrews as "the brightness of God's glory and the express image of his person"; in Second Corinthians as "the image of God"; in Colossians as "the image of the invisible God." St. John quotes Jesus as saying, "He that hath seen me hath seen the Father." So to be committed to God is to be committed to Jesus Christ. As St. Paul says, "Ye are Christ's, and Christ is God's." So the question is, Are you satisfied with God's likeness as you see it in Jesus Christ? Are you content with this bargain that you have made? Are you quite at ease to remember, every new morning of your life, that you are pledged to His sole loyalty throughout all time and eternity? Is that all right with you? Remembering everything it implies and entails, remembering its discipline, its duties and its restrictions, remembering all the things you must do because you are His, and perhaps especially remembering the things you are never going to do again because you are His, remembering the Cross, can you still say: "As for me, I shall be satisfied, each morning that I awake, with thy likeness?"

3. But there is still a third way in which the words "When I awake" may be taken. They may be taken as referring to the resurrection morn, and understood to mean, "When I wake up from the sleep of death into another life." Modern commentators are agreed that that cannot have been what the Psalmist originally meant, and I am sure they are right, but that is how the words have been understood, especially by ordinary folk, throughout most of Christian history. That meaning, therefore, has at least been hallowed by long Christian use.

The New Testament constantly reminds us that in this life we have for the most part to walk by faith rather than by sight, trusting in a God whom no man hath seen at any time. Yet it always goes on to speak of another life, the life eternal, in which faith will give place to open vision; so that, as St. Paul says, we shall see no longer through a glass darkly but rather face to face, knowing God even as we are known by Him; and as St. John says, we shall see Him as He is.

What is it going to be like? What vision will meet our surprised eyes as we waken to eternal life? How much of what went before will be swept away, and how much will seem rather to be fulfilled? Will anything at all of the familiar earthly pattern be conserved? Shall we recognize the friends we have made here? Shall we resume our family relationships? To none of these questions can we give confident answers. Death is a bourne from which no traveller returns to give us tidings. Or if any have returned, they have been silent.

> When Lazarus left his charnel-cave,
>   And home to Mary's house return'd
>   Was this demanded—if he yearn'd
> To hear her weeping at his grave?
>
> 'Where went thou, brother, those four days?'
>   There lives no record of reply,
>   Which telling what it is to die
> Had surely added praise to praise. . . .
>
> Behold a man raised up by Christ!
>   The rest remaineth unrevealed;
>   He told it not; or something sealed
> The lips of the Evangelist.

Not even the most learned philosopher or theologian knows what it is going to be like. But there is one thing which the simplest Christian knows—he knows it is going to be all right. Somewhere, somewhen, somehow we who are worshipping God here will wake up to see Him as He is, and face to face; but where or when we know not, or even whether it will be in a "where" and a "when," that is, in space and time at all. No doubt it will all be utterly different from anything we have ever imagined or thought about it. No doubt God Himself will be unimaginably different from all our present conceptions of Him. But He will be unimaginably different only because He will be unimaginably better. The only thing we do certainly know is that our highest hopes will be more than fulfilled, and our deepest longings more than gratified. We can be certain that there will be nothing to disappoint, however much there may be to surprise. Thus each of us can say with this Psalmist: "As for me, I will behold thy face in righteousness: I shall be satisfied, when I awake, with thy likeness."

It looks, then, as if it did not greatly matter which of the three awakenings the Psalmist had in mind—whether he meant awaking from a fit of depression to a juster estimate of values, or awaking from sleep every morning to the light of a new day, or the great awakening of resurrection morning. It does not much matter, because the essential confidence which he expresses would in each case be the same. It is the confidence expressed by many other Psalmists. "He satisfieth the longing soul, and filleth the hungry soul with goodness." "Thou openest thine hand, and satisfiest the desire of every living thing."

And the lesson for us is also the same. Are you really quite happy about this great trust that you have reposed in Christ? Are you content, if you will allow the well-worn phrase, to have placed all your eggs in this one basket? Remember it is only out of complete submission that complete confidence can ever arise. Your assurance of *His* trustworthiness can grow only in proportion to *your* willingness to trust Him. But if you do give Him your whole heart, quite unashamedly owning Him, and following Him without reserve, content to bear His reproach as well as to enjoy His companionship, then it is certain that every time you wake up to remember Him, you will be satisfied with His likeness. And as to the last awakening, you will be able to sing with Isaac Watts and with St. Paul:

> I know that safe with Him remains
>   Protected by His power
> What I've committed to His trust
>   Till the decisive hour.
>
> Then will He own His servant's name
>   Before the Father's face,
> And in the new Jerusalem
>   Appoint my soul a place.

BOOKS BY JOHN BAILLIE

The Roots of Religion in the Human Soul (New York: Doran; London: Hodder & Stoughton, 1926)

The Interpretation of Religion (New York: Charles Scribner's Sons, 1928; Edinburgh: T. & T. Clark, 1929)

The Place of Jesus Christ in Modern Christianity (New York: Charles Scribner's Sons; Edinburgh: T. & T. Clark, 1929)

And the Life Everlasting (New York: Charles Scribner's Sons, 1933; London: Oxford University Press, 1934)

A Diary of Private Prayer (New York: Charles Scribner's Sons; London: Oxford University Press, 1937)

Our Knowledge of God (New York: Charles Scribner's Sons; London: Oxford University Press, 1939)

Invitation to Pilgrimage (New York: Charles Scribner's Sons; London: Oxford University Press, 1942)

The Prospects of Spiritual Renewal (London: Oxford University Press, 1943)

What is Christian Civilization? (New York: Charles Scribner's Sons; London: Christophers, 1945)

The Mind of the Modern University (University Pamphlets Series, London: S.C.M. Press, 1946)

Spiritual Religion (London: Allen & Unwin, n.d.? 1947)

The Belief in Progress (New York: Charles Scribner's Sons; London: Oxford University Press, 1950)

The Human Situation (William Ainslie Memorial Lecture, London: Longmans, Green & Co., 1950)

Natural Science and the Spiritual Life (British Association Lecture, New York: Charles Scribner's Sons, 1952; London: Oxford University Press, 1951)

A Diary of Readings (edited, New York: Charles Scribner's Sons; London: Oxford University Press, 1955)

The Idea of Revelation in Recent Thought (London: Oxford University Press, 1956)

POSTHUMOUSLY PUBLISHED:

The Sense of the Presence of God (Gifford Lectures for 1961–62. New York: Charles Scribner's Sons; London: Oxford University Press, 1962)

Christian Devotion (New York: Charles Scribner's Sons; London: Oxford University Press, 1962)

INDEX